House on the River

A Summer Journey

House on the River

NESSA RAPOPORT

HARMONY BOOKS ⬥ NEW YORK

Essays previously published in the *Los Angeles Times Book Review,*
The Jewish Week, and *Re://collections* appear here in slightly altered form,
as does a brief excerpt from *Preparing for Sabbath.*

I am grateful to the Canada Council for the Arts for its generosity.

Published by Harmony Books, New York, New York. Member of
the Crown Publishing Group, a division of Random House, Inc.
www.crownpublishing.com

HARMONY BOOKS is a registered trademark and the Harmony
Books colophon is a trademark of Random House, Inc.

Printed in the United States of America

DESIGN BY BARBARA STURMAN

Library of Congress Cataloging-in-Publication Data
Rapoport, Nessa.
    House on the river: a summer journey/ by Nessa Rapoport. — 1st ed.
      p. cm.
    1. Rapoport, Nessa — Travel — Ontario. 2. Authors, American —
20th century — Family relationships. 3. Trent-Severn Waterway
(Ont.) — Description and travel. 4. Boats and boating — Ontario —
Trent-Severn Waterway. 5. Authors, American — 20th century —
Biography. 6. Ontario — Social life and customs. 7. Rapoport,
Nessa — Family. 8. Houseboats — Ontario. 9. Family — Ontario.
I. Title.
    PS3568.A627H68 2004
    818'.5403 — dc22   2003025240

ISBN 1-4000-4887-7

10 9 8 7 6 5 4 3 2 1
First Edition

For my parents and my sisters

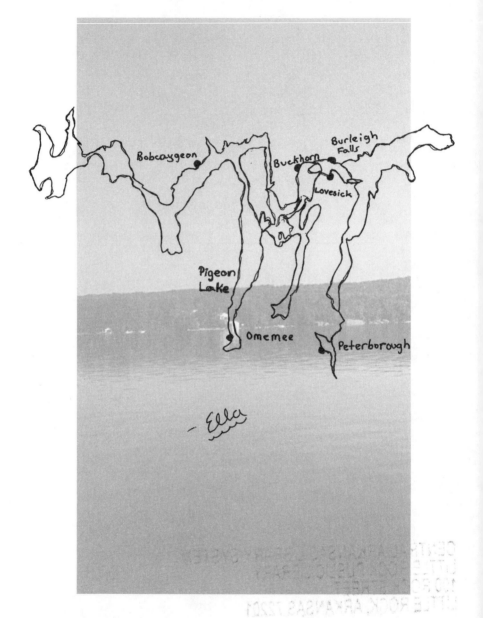

Bobcaygeon

Buckhorn

Burleigh Falls

Lovesick

Pigeon Lake

Omemee

Peterborough

— Ella

CONTENTS

"Make it a book to soothe the soul."

—JAKE

The Boat Trip

Sunday

I AM STEERING THE BOAT through unfamiliar water, translucent columns of lavender and silver. We are alone on the lake at the end of summer. The vast sky, the low horizon, are a homecoming, but the shimmering opal light is nothing I have seen in Canada. The rare enchantment of this pale, floating world will soon transmute into the blue lake fringed with evergreen that is the essence of our summer memory. We have talked for years of the boat trip, and now the landscapes are slipping by.

Ten years ago, in 1987, my uncle Nat and aunt Ora rented a houseboat to travel with their children through the locks of the Trent-Severn Waterway in Ontario. Their journey ended at Bobcaygeon, the town where for fifty years my grandparents, uncles, and mother, and then my generation of cousins, spent summers lounging about the ramshackle cottage that in my imagination continues to represent paradise.

Each fall since then, my uncle would say to me wistfully, "Maybe next summer we'll go on the boat trip." Last December, I realized that he was over seventy. If we did not go soon, the trip would remain a dream.

With us on this journey are my mother and my children. At nine and five, Jake and Ella are finally old enough to be safe on a boat but not too old to disdain the idea of a week with their family. Within me is my third child, whose anticipated birth in the coming winter sealed my decision to go.

Why has the phrase "the boat trip" held me for a decade in its thrall? Why does travel on a rented houseboat seem the most sublime of voyages? And how have I come to be a writer whose family and past — from which I fled — are increasingly replenishing?

My escape from Toronto, my determination to forge a life away from my birthplace, to inhabit a world more operatic than placid Canada, has returned me in the middle of my life to the place where I began. Not to the pinched, puritanical winter of the city, but to a Sabbath of plenitude, my heart's sanctuary.

"Many waters cannot quench love," declares Solomon's Song, an invisible banner unfurling above me.

Standing on the deck this first day, I am shocked by pleasure. I proclaim my allegiance to urban intensity, but this landscape is, like poetry, the seeming luxury that turns out to be essential. I want to memorize not what I see — which unfolds, extends, retreats second to second — but its effect on my body, refurbished by ease and sensuality.

The boat moves up Pigeon Lake, one of the Kawartha Lakes that span the province. Beyond us, the Muskoka region has the grandeur of the true north. But I love the Kawarthas, wilderness domesticated, tamed. The forests do not seem primordial. The lakes are of a civilized scale. Twenty years after fleeing Canada for the swooping majesty of New York, I can savor a water journey with the shore always in view.

In Manhattan, the blue geometries of sky wedged between brick buildings are glorious and sufficient. The morning sun gilds the pediments as I walk. I do not long for nature; I remain as entranced by the charge of New York as I did when I was a child and first encountered the city, looking up at the march of skyscrapers, the colossal department stores.

On the lake, however, most of what I see is light. How expansive it seems after the round of winter. For I am a changeling, a voluptuary of summer born in an icy land. From September until May I pined for the long days, a connoisseur who could divine the quotient of sunlight from a sliver of dawn at the edge of the bedroom shade, who huddled at the vent near the floor, waiting for the reassuring hum of the furnace as if it were salvation.

The exclamations of my family dissolve the reverie. We have reached shore instead of the channel toward which we were blithely heading. Much laughter ensues, as we are forced to navigate more humbly. The elation of mistakes without consequence. What is the hurry?

My uncle teaches my son and daughter to steer. His even temperament is a quality I cherish in my mother's family. I, like my father and his kin, am of a more passionate and less adaptable nature. As a child, I felt as if the entire alphabet of emotion were available to me at any instant, while my mother hovered permanently between *L* and *M*. In my forties, however, I have met complexities beyond any I could contrive. As a result, I am a tentative pilgrim to the prospects of tranquility.

Nat is the eldest of my mother's four brothers, and, like all my uncles, has an undisguised weakness for children. Watching him patiently explain how to maneuver the boat among the buoys, or smooth the oversized page of the map to show Jake and Ella where we are, I am a child, looking up at him expectantly, and an old woman, recalling joy. This tripled consciousness — now and then and after — does not impede but amplifies my delight.

Where are the other men? My husband, an artist, is working to meet commission deadlines in New York. My father, while encouraging, is constitutionally incapable of taking a trip for six days in cramped quarters where our mode of operation must be improvised.

From the start we have the lakes and rivers to ourselves. One week before Labor Day, holiday time is almost past for Canadians, who are, in their thrifty fashion, preparing for autumn.

I, however, cleave to summer — the stately processional of small islands with red-roofed cottages and matching whitewashed boathouses, stands of graceful trees whose branches overhang the water, weathered docks from which children are diving, their squeals reaching us with an immediacy that belies the distance. Objectively, the sights are pretty rather than beautiful. But for us there is nothing objective about the boat trip.

We are journeying to Bobcaygeon. Not toward it, for we will travel east to Peterborough and then loop back, passing through Pigeon Lake again, north and west from where we began, in order to reach the town that is the destination of this voyage. Intuitively, we do not talk about it. I am not the only one who has resolved to relish our meandering and be wary of expectation. My cousins have told me that the town is overbuilt, ruined. The cottage was torn down, and my grandmother is gone.

I do not believe that such facts signify. The house has lived within me all these years, and as soon as I think of my grandmother, she stands in her dress the color of the sky, waiting behind the screen door for us to arrive, for the scrape of our car on the gravel as we pull up before the Sabbath.

My cousins and I race into the house to change. In minutes we are jumping into the river, crying out as the water embraces us, daring each other to the next dock and back while my uncle, unencumbered by any acquaintance with ecology, shampoos his hair in contentment.

My grandmother calls us in to candlelighting, to the ravishment of Friday night dinner, challah too soft to cut, brisket flaking, potatoes drenched in gravy, lemon cake and brownies and apple pie as dusk turns to night. The cottage is falling apart, undemanding. Our parents are not here, and so there is no one to afflict our adolescence with an effort to improve us. Long after everyone else is sleeping, after my grandmother's ponderous steps up the painted red stairs, after the Sabbath clock has shut the one remaining reading light, I tiptoe onto the screened porch and shiver into my bed, waiting fraught moments until my body warms the sheets.

Outside, the trees whisper benignly. An occasional car light sweeps across me, magnifying the dark. My self-scrutiny relents, and I plummet into dense, sweet sleep. When I wake, I can see the wild grasses, the pale orange and mauve flowers grazing the screens that are the only barrier between me and the day.

We have nothing to do, those magical words. I lie on the dock, dreaming. In the cracks between the worn wood planks, quicksilver minnows flash in the underlight. I turn over to watch beneath closing lids as my cousins dive fearlessly, again and again, into the river.

Squinting into the noon glare, I see, toward Pigeon Lake, the green boathouse with white trim that seems to wait for our recognition each summer, as if it would disappear unless we fixed it in our gaze. We think we will always be at the cottage and that the boathouse, evergreen as the water beneath it, will persist stolidly, enduring forever.

All day, pleasure boats pass us in a stately procession, as layered in decks and brass fixtures as the most ornate wedding cakes. We utter the word "yacht" with reverence, for we long to be aboard one of these confections. The skippers wave, their children scurrying while they stay responsibly at the helm.

Across the river, an expanse of plush lawn curves down to the water. Perched upon it is a greenhouse, panes glittering like diamonds. In my imagination saturated with fairy tales, the house on the lawn is an estate from a sorcerer's kingdom. There is never anyone on the emerald grass, or in the greenhouse, or on the dock, alluringly mirroring ours but across, beyond, away. Even when we are old enough to swim to the opposite bank of the river, the mysterious magic of the house on the lawn is not dispelled. I love to close my eyes, the radiant sphere of sun engraved on black, and then startle myself when I look upon a world that is for an instant richer and deeper.

Lunch is almost too much effort. Only after my grandmother's mild exhortation do we climb the stone steps, leaving abruptly the blazing midday for the dim cottage. After we eat, my aunts and uncles retreat into sleep. My cousins disappear. I close the screen door gently behind me to saunter toward town, past the bend in the road, past the slip where a car checks my path to back up inch by inch until the motorboat it has been hauling is eased onto the water. I stroll by Gordon's marina and then Edgar's, where we buy our milk and store in a freezer vault the kosher meat brought from Toronto.

Near the sign that says "Front Street," beyond Locust Lodge, is an empty stone trough studded with iron rings where once horses stopped to drink. Crossing one bridge, then another, past the post office, shuttered against the heat, I thread my way along the swing bridge toward the library.

There I will pass the hours in communion with books I have already read, as my mother did before me. The Bobcaygeon library is redolent with their intoxicating scent, musty from river and summer. Its battered wood tables, towering stacks, and shadowy corners receive me with timeless patience. I see my mother as a young girl, loving the Nancy Drew books as I love the bodice-rippers showcased here unashamedly. Miss Cosh is no longer the librarian, but her name has entered the family lore.

When I look up, it is twilight and I must hurry back, in time to hear one uncle or another say the prayer that separates day from night, the Sabbath day from all others. On the weekend of my sixteenth birthday, driving after Shabbat to buy soft ice cream, we hear on the radio that an astronaut has landed on the moon.

Often at night my grandmother takes a last walk by the river. Sometimes I keep her company, although we do not talk much. My grandmother is self-sufficient. She has a magisterial mind and a cool, anti-psychological disposition. To me, there is something restful in her dispassion. I am grateful that her unquenched curiosity about the world does not extend to her blood relations. My grandmother is a receptive listener.

In August, she might point to the moon's globe refracted in water or note the chill of autumn. The light that reaches us tonight descends from stars that died aeons ago. These are the kinds of facts my grandmother knows. Alone with her, each in solitude, I am not yet conscious of how much I love her.

The unwinding hours of late Friday afternoon until our sated departure will be jewels I restring continually. When, in winter, I cannot sleep, I recite the tactile inventory—the air spiced with pine, the slap of our bare feet on porch boards, the murmur of the river against the dock, the smell of heat on the mesh of the screen door. The harmony of those Sabbaths was not, nor would be for many years, in my emotional repertoire.

To entice me on the boat trip, Ora conjured lazy days of reading while we drifted through the pastoral waters of my youth. Now I accuse her of misleading me. On the trip Nat and Ora made a decade ago, there were several cousins on board, teenagers who were delighted to take charge of navigation. Today we all need to work. We are fewer hands with a surprising amount to do. Books languish as we concentrate on our course.

The sky has resumed its azure hue, the land its green intensity. Only my uncle notices the hour. Ora, I discover, has a worse sense of direction than I do and is content to trust the family crew. My mother, having organized my father's schedule, meals, and nightly calls, has left her lists determinedly behind. And the children, like all children, have the gift of looking neither forward nor back.

Time is becoming pliant, the boat's passage gauged only by the changing numbers on the buoys. When we reach Buckhorn at four o'clock, there is not a hint of dusk in the glazed sky. A delicious languor possesses me; I cannot stop yawning.

"Slow" instructs a prominent sign.

Although we try cutting the engine as we approach the lock, we almost crash into a docked pleasure boat. Its owners' faces are transformed in seconds from hospitality to alarm. In our panicky effort to avoid collision, we spin around full circle. Finally, with the help of nautical veterans ashore, we succeed in tying up at the lock.

I am no longer sleepy.

This is the first of several occasions when my mother will express her relief that my father is not here to witness our fiascoes. A lover of slapstick, he will enjoy the journey far more in narrative than in the uncertainty of experience. Before he retired, my father was an academic physician of repute, who, like others of his stature, required a degree of placating at home in order to launch himself daily into the world. In the dominion of such men, accidents do not simply happen, as an intrinsic dimension of nature. No, when something goes awry, aspersions must be cast.

Although my maternal uncles shared with my father the quality of moral ambition, they did not have his turbulent perfectionism. They carried their innate gifts lightly — and excelled at sitting around the kitchen table, snacking and laughing, while my father was more likely to be sequestered in the den, immersed in medical journals, available for the big conversations but disengaged from the trivialities that constitute family life.

On the morning of our departure, Nat was punctual, ready to get the proverbial early start. But when he could not galvanize the rest of us, the angriest he became was to say with resignation, "Are we ever going on a trip?"

When I was a child, our family's early starts were achieved infrequently, and then under considerable strain. That within a half hour of our triumphant departure today we traveled with aplomb in the opposite direction of our route, unaware that we were lost, and that our entry into Buckhorn has been near catastrophic to the maritime property of those in our immediate vicinity, elicits in Nat an amiable rue. By tonight it will be funny. I can already imagine how we will tell the story, unable to finish our sentences.

Nevertheless, we disembark gingerly, afraid to face the more adept travelers berthed nearby. Buckhorn's temporary inhabitants do not seem to bear a grudge.

A serene peace prevails as the afternoon deepens. My mother and aunt are thrilled by the presence of impeccable bathrooms at the lock, replete with both hot and potable water. And I am entranced by the assumption, which I attribute without evidence to Canadian literacy, that visitors are expected to know the word "potable."

Alongside the canal is a small, open-air restaurant with take-out ice cream, flavors inscribed in script on a wooden board. I scan the sign for "mint chocolate chip," which I associate with the long-ago summer holidays my grandmother recalled for me in satisfyingly idle exchanges on the porch. I hardly remember my grandfather, who died the summer I turned five, but I know he courted my grandmother in Bobcaygeon.

Walking along the cement banks, I feel myself slough off anxiety: the trepidation with which, at forty-four, I embarked on this pregnancy for a longed-for third child, praying that we would see her well into adulthood; the illness of my mother's brother Rafe, my beloved youngest uncle, afflicted with cancer that seemed cured but has reemerged malignantly; and my father's failing memory, with the unknown it augurs. These are the shadow companions of our journey.

At midlife I am trying to accept that henceforth all joy will be dappled. Yet as day turns to evening, I am pristinely happy. The smell of gasoline, of barbecue, even, faintly, of sewage, invokes Bobcaygeon, for which I have longed since I said good-bye to the cottage with Rafe twenty-two years ago. How often have I wished to return for even a single day. I have traveled to many countries and lived abroad, forsaking the provinces of Canada. And yet the cottage has been my inner destination.

In my forties, I am fascinated by the way life can circle upon itself, reacquainting me unexpectedly with old friends who shaped me, with men I loved painfully for whom I now feel only gratitude, and at last, this very week, with the place that symbolizes the possibility that we imperfect creatures can find true repose.

The tidy houses of Buckhorn perched on symmetrical lawns seem classically Canadian. Although I have embraced America with its risks and largesse, the modesty of this country, once gleefully rejected, feels like shelter. I am relieved not to be looking over my shoulder.

When I moved to New York in the 1970s, I was oblivious to the bankruptcy of the city, to the subsequent crack epidemic and the crime it engendered. I proudly mastered which block — even which side of the block — was safe and which to skirt. My friends and I amused ourselves by watching cockroaches scatter when we turned on a light.

Now our family's two-bedroom apartment sells for the price of a mansion in the suburbs — but we are still wed to the city. I have an immigrant's love for New York that cannot be diluted by the tantalizing prospect of sufficient closets or an immediate college savings account. I joke that I am post-bourgeois, citing a civic thinker who contends that in great cities the walls of private residences are porous. As New Yorkers, we do not insulate ourselves in mammoth fortresses but sally forth at any hour into the vibrant street.

For Jake and Ella, however, Canada is the exotic land. They pose for photographs at the base of a soaring flagpole, then tip back their heads to see the red maple leaf against the pure sky. This is the country of their mother before she met Dad, an era remote and inaccessible. They are American children, born into a culture that has hegemony across the globe, whereas I was raised in the forgotten world of the Commonwealth, when Canada was legally a part of the British Empire, Queen Elizabeth my queen and the Union Jack my flag. I read books about boys called Colin and Edmund, Leslie and Vivian, or girls named Winifred and Gwendolyn.

Among the duties of parenthood I relish is the cultivation of memory. I have given Jake and Ella transparent envelopes containing markers, a blank journal, and an instant camera, promising that they can buy postcards at every mooring. While we shop for groceries in Buckhorn, Jake and Ella deliberate over their selections fastidiously. I assure them we have all the time in the world. I have not forgotten that when Ella first learned to speak, she horrified me by asking at random moments, "Are we out of time?" This journey is an experiment in ignoring the taunt of the workday's receding finish line.

For supper, we return to the boat, attempting to kindle the barbecue on deck with an ineptitude to which we are already accustomed. In the fragrant smoke of other people's dinners we impotently click the lighter, joking about our going to bed hungry.

At last a local boat owner offers us a reprieve. Naturally, he lights the gas in an instant. Without comment, we add this episode to the cache: the wrong direction, the fumbled steering, the barbecue.

Food deferred tastes even better. Everyone devours the vegetable burgers purchased by my mother. For her, the family's high priestess of food's relationship to health, there is no vacation from nutrition. My sisters and I know all about protein, carbohydrates, and cholesterol. At family gatherings, to my mother's dismay, we eat chocolate bars and potato chips.

All of us clean up scrupulously, outdoing each other in good citizenship on this first day, determined to keep the boat "shipshape" — a word, new to Ella, that she repeats with satisfaction.

The chaos of modern life — the proliferation of forms, passwords, solicitations by phone and mail — is a daily threat to clarity. On a boat there is room only for what is useful. I am a failed minimalist and love the imposed restraint. Each latched cupboard in a clever place suits my desire to pare down, to rid myself of the clutter I have unwittingly amassed and am not ruthless enough to discard. My life in New York is a jumble of the children's favorite toys, of indecipherable crayon on newsprint saved for posterity.

I have not succeeded in emulating the women I admire who part with the sentimental detritus of family life without a qualm. Instead, I have removed myself from the unceasing self-reproach to organize: On the boat there are neither objects nor papers. I am, briefly, free.

One evening a week in New York, I leave my job not for home but for my studio, where I resume my solitude. In my small room, computer screen a luminous object of meditation, I dream in syllables. Around me are letters, books, boxed baby clothes I am saving for my grandchildren, thirty journals inscribed since I was eighteen, cabinets containing everything I have written.

Here I lived for five years before I married, with a

bed, a bookcase, and a desk as my companions. High over the city in a room of my own, only the sky in my window and a view of the river from my desk, alone with my anxieties about the unknown future and the dissonance between my imagined life and the life I led, I was so captivated by the unimpeded southern light that I hung no shades or curtains. I changed my clothes behind an open closet door and fell asleep each night opposite the soothing darkness, which said to me: You will not always live this life. You will find the one in whom your soul delights.

The quest for love consumed me, for it had to be Jewish love, embracing worldliness and Sabbath feasts, travel to foreign climes and a gleaming table around which sat cherished friends — and children. A life of uncompromising alliance with art but also stability, a moral and tactile life, of honor and sensuality. With whom would I invent it?

During the years in my studio, I did not return often to Canada. As I began to earn a living and was rewarded increasingly, I submerged my pride in worry. "Youth is wasted on the young," I chastised myself, to no avail. In the lobby of my building, which had once been a hotel and consisted mostly of single rooms, were women who were middle-aged or older, who lived alone, venturing forth in inclement weather to shop for groceries purposefully and then more haltingly with cane or walker.

Lord, I would say as I lay in my bed looking out at the night, do not let me die in this room.

Now, of course, the room is my sole harbor from a life so dense with all I desired that the minute I turn the key, my past, even its pain, welcomes me, filtered through the bounty of the present day, anguish tempered by compassion for my younger self, and, occasionally, a strange wistfulness for that unremitting fervor.

At other times, even a room of my own is insufficient. I am defeated by the unfilled needs of the workday, the phone calls about the children's school arrangements that jangle me from my reverie, the seduction of rewriting my to-do list instead of straining to hear an ebbing muse. When I am not writing, the hands of the clock accelerate to rebuke me. In the city, only my writing has the capacity to vanquish time. Before the screen I am as contemplative as the most adept recluse, scant minutes miraculously supple enough to encompass whatever must be said or left unsaid.

Sometimes I play the music of my past, the records I heard first in the summer I turned sixteen. That year I was handmaiden to my friend Rose's secret love. Rose was an artist, silent and ethereally lovely, masses of yellow hair falling down her back in unruly splendor. Her courtier had a charisma whose vigor seemed subversive. She fair, he swarthy, they were the virgin and the gypsy, and I, observing, dazzled by the beauty and foreshadowing of their doomed love, was the privileged witness. Rose is the daughter of survivors of the Holocaust. The magnetic boy who adored her was Jewish, but not of a European Orthodox family, his long hair an emblem of the youth culture so alien to her parents' path. Their romance was the fulfillment of my imagining and theirs, nobility made pungent by desire.

The opening chord of certain songs revives the mourning of my early adolescence, the season before agency when a young woman could mouth the truths of feminism but not yet embody them, so architectonic was the foundation of her girlhood, whose lesson was that to be the object of desire was desire's end, suffering equated with devotion. It was not possible then to imagine well-being without romantic love or to choose experience for its own sake and find it sufficient.

My weekends in Bobcaygeon were an unexpected retreat from my cruelty to myself. In my longing to cast off Toronto and my inchoate dissatisfaction with everything, I could not anticipate that summer weekends spent without the salvation of friends, in the company of my grandmother, assorted uncles and aunts, and younger cousins, would be Eden.

Outside, in Buckhorn's blue dusk, I call my husband in his studio. Only an hour away by plane, New York already seems strange. I am not able to describe, holding the receiver as I watch the vault of sky retain the last light, the effect of this first day, saying only, "It is all I wanted."

I wish you were with us, I tell him, before putting the children on the phone. But then I wonder: Could Tobi imagine himself into our past, into what might seem to anyone else mundane? For my uncle, my mother, and me, each place, each name, is resonant with our history.

Tobi's parents and grandparents are refugees from Germany. Like millions of twentieth-century Jews, they saw their houses and land confiscated and then destroyed. One grandmother was a cosseted child in Frankfurt, then a wealthy young wife on a skiing vacation in Switzerland the day that Hitler was elected chancellor. She refused to return home; prophesying calamity, she forfeited a world to save her family. The other grandmother's first-born son, only daughter, and first grandson were murdered by the Nazis.

My grandmother, by virtue of her birth in Canada in 1897, was already exceptional. That four generations of our family spent summers in the same cottage was another distinctive feature of the Jewish-Canadian culture my grandparents invented, a culture I inherited unselfconsciously. How did we turn out this way?

At nightfall, we pull the curtains across the windows and hunker down, we tell ourselves, impressed by our ability to deploy the colloquial. Although the boat purportedly sleeps eight, we four adults and two children can scarcely manage. My aunt and uncle are crammed onto a narrow pullout couch in the front, with my mother occupying the second, a handbreadth away. Directed by Jake, we have constructed a double bed out of the facing dining room benches, with a bunk on top that pulls down from the ceiling ingeniously.

No one wants to sleep there. None of the grown-ups (a category from which I exclude myself) are willing, because, as they indicate obliquely, they have reached the age when they cannot manage without using the bathroom at least once. My daughter is too young to be without guardrails. I am pregnant and hardly limber, with the same constraint as the adults. And my son is adamant that he cannot sleep on top; there are bugs in the window screens.

Faced with the refusal of other candidates, however, he grudgingly consents to try.

At four in the morning, all of us but Ella are awake, giggling as, one after another, we traipse with flashlights to the bathroom.

Woozy with fatigue, I am sympathetic to Jake's plea to help him go back to sleep. I reach into the bunk to stroke his hair, awash with tenderness.

Although he can hardly speak, he insists he will be up for hours. "Keep in touch," he enjoins me drowsily.

"It's your great-aunt and -uncle who are keeping in touch," says my mother. Beneath her prim delivery is a double entendre in waiting.

I will not forget the sound of my family's laughter in the middle of the night, protecting me as I lie awake, listening.

Monday

A WAY. AWAY FROM CUSTOM, from labor, away from the unceasing admonition of my desk: Attend to me. Away from habits of sleep and waking, we are closer to our true nature, a constellation of organisms, realigning lyrically without plan or end.

Cradled by water, we do not need to maintain the illusion of solidity. We float in and out of time, toward a future that was our past. On the boat trip, the past is not discrete or tidy. It does not stay where we consigned it or unspool by invitation. Instead, what we remember is anarchic, whimsical, reappearing when we thought we'd said farewell, or refusing even the most delectable lure. Nat, my mother, and I barter memories when they choose to emerge and greet amiably the souvenirs of others — my uncle Rafe, my grandmother.

Half a century ago, in endless summer, a teenage girl named Bridget paddled her canoe past the dock of the cottage, back and forth on the Bobcaygeon River. In a white bathing suit, blond hair to her waist, she was an icon of loveliness. Decades later, Rafe would evoke the vision of Bridget, to my aunt Nina's bemusement and my fascination: What kind of allure could be sustained beyond time?

For Rose and me, romantic love was the only theater grand enough for the scale of our imaginations. In the apprenticeship of girlhood, Rose and I waited. We read books about love and fashioned our inner lives accordingly, but waiting was our task.

Rose was sixteen when her great love appeared. He recognized her, and she, favored, chosen above all others, became spellbinding. In the peak of the next summer, as Rose had promised, I was waylaid by a first love as momentous and galvanic as hers. Suddenly, I knew the impact of my body, dipped in sun, abruptly beautiful.

No matter how old we become, Rose and I will always return within to the beautiful girl of that year, the season when each of us — first Rose, then I — stopped waiting. We do not want to replicate her, through surgery or artifice; we want to inhabit her, feel again the thrilling vitality conferred not by the gaze of men, as it was then, but by our own sanction. Finding our moxie, Rose calls it: the juice, the succulence of being alive.

Because I lived beneath the leaden skies of a northern city while coveting a trustworthy Mediterranean sun, I have always been intrigued by weather. On a boat trip, the weather is not an opening platitude but a legitimate subject of conversation. Almost incidental in New York, it is at the heart of our preoccupations this morning, for we woke to the random clicking of rain on the decks and roof. The mutability of the elements is determining: Will we crowd together inside the boat, venturing onto the deck in clammy raincoats only to approach or leave a lock, vistas blurry, navigator peering to discern the buoys? Or will the gods oblige these bumbling mariners with rain at night and dawn's clearing?

By breakfast a hot light is pouring over us. Sweaters and sweatshirts litter the couches, ready to be donned if the weather turns again, for the sun is fleeting. A wind arises and clouds are strewn across the heavens. The air is dank, then balmy, then bracing. Like old salts, we peer into the distance, relishing our speculation.

All of us are in love with the names we pass, Lovesick Lake, Fantasy Island, Clear Lake, in love with the smell of fresh water and cedar, the motor's companionable rumble beneath us.

We are maneuvering among red buoys, past toy islands, Jake with the binoculars calling out the numbers to my mother, who is steering.

"C221," he says. "C222."

Suddenly he cries, "Man your places. Man your battle posts."

"Sunken island," Ora points out. "On your right."

We have reached Burleigh Falls, Jake announces. "Going down low," he calls out. "Get ready."

One day into the trip, he has figured out how to cut the motor to enter the lock "dead slow," turn off the fridge's power, knot the rope or loop it around the horizontal cables spanning the mossy walls in preparation for our rising or falling. Already we have delegated these tasks to him. He is far more nimble than we are at leaping, with a gymnast's compact grace, from deck to shore, his hands adept at the figure eight that secures the boat.

In New York, like most middle-class children, he has no domestic responsibilities except contrived ones. On the boat trip he is not only useful but indispensable. My uncle's praise, my mother's gratitude, light his already expressive face. Ella, too, can help, wielding the metal post with which we push off.

In their orange life jackets and Blue Jay caps,

they look nautical. My daughter, however, retains a distinctive Manhattan originality: She has elected to spend the day in her pajamas. The life jacket over her print sleepwear exhibits a certain who-cares flair. In the reflective light of sky and river her eyes are a color I do not see in the city, a blue so resplendent that I am startled each time she turns to me.

A houseboat lettered *Happy Days* drives by. I am surpassingly happy, trying to memorize the texture of each minute, convinced I shall not know such a time again, an oasis of untainted plenty. The jackals that await us bay only distantly, at the perimeter of consciousness. Now I am empty of worry as I step into the galley.

My aunt and mother were the food committee, checking their shopping lists with each other in the weeks preceding our rendezvous in Toronto. Ora's virtue as a relative is manifest in the fact that while we were stowing our clothes on the boat, she was finding the most convenient cupboard in which to place her bags of miniature Peanut Chews.

My aunt, it emerges, does not eat anything for breakfast that resembles real food. Lanky as a dancer, she prefers the pieces of muffin and candy that issue from her luggage, to the children's amazement. Although I, as my mother's daughter, have raised Jake and Ella with a precocious knowledge of nutrition, I remember the incomparable taste of the sugared cereal my grandmother gave us willingly every Sabbath morning in Bobcaygeon and am pleased by this transgression of their assumptions.

Our gourmet lunch consists of canned tomato soup and crackers, ornamented by cheese slices that have been carefully arranged by my son and daughter. My mother tries to infiltrate some fruit and vegetables into this menu, but we are content. Afterward, Ella stretches on the couch luxuriantly. "For me," she proclaims, "doing nothing is doing something."

The boat confers on daily life a profound stillness, an unexpected antidote to genetic impatience. Why rush? The first two days of the trip have had, despite the necessary bustle, a Sabbath dreaminess, rest rather than holiday in the conventional sense, ample time, enough to talk to each other and trail off, to read to the children or look out the window.

Only now, in the brilliant early afternoon, do we flag, squinting against the obdurate light.

My uncle naps. Although he is nearly seventy-two, he will always be spry in my eyes. I can read the signs of age on his face, but his body is lean: My mother's family has a severe antipathy to fat, conveniently buttressed by genes. Nat is the uncle who sent every niece and nephew a birthday card until we were well into our twenties; who could, as a child, tell the day of the week for any date within a century.

My uncles are great cardplayers, board game masters, joke tellers. I take for granted their skill in navigation, chess, and numbers. In my own family, it is my mother who manages the finances and investments, pays the bills, and prepares the tax returns. Her facility with numbers is so apparent that her accountant periodically offers her a job.

According to my unified theory of relations, as long as one member of a clan has a particular aptitude, why should I strain to approximate it? The gifts of my mother and her brothers are so natural we do not take note of them. Only when someone marries in are we startled to learn that not everyone belongs to a family that deems "between you and I" a sin; not everyone fills the time between ordering and eating at a restaurant by scribbling on the paper tablecloth possible solutions to a math conundrum.

Of course, they are the children of my grandmother. In the twentieth century, a great cultural fuss was made of the growing divide between art and science. My grandmother, coming of age in the Edwardian era of colonial Canada, had a mind that could shuttle effortlessly between Thomas Hardy and the theory of relativity.

The oldest of ten children, she was a "flash," the slang applied to her at the turn of the twentieth century. From her earliest years she excelled in school. Her grandchildren knew she had read all of Shakespeare by the time she was twelve.

Bub, as we called her, had a mind that seemed to retain everything she read or heard. She might quote a lively conversation conducted with a stranger while she was on her European honeymoon in 1924, recite a cherished poem by Tennyson, or use a witticism devised inadvertently by the woman who helped her in the house when her children were young.

For nearly thirty years, she wrote and broadcast her commentary on the CBC, Canada's national radio, on a program devoted to women's issues called *Trans-Canada Matinee*. When I was growing up, we had in our house a recording Bub made in April 1943. In a country where, it emerged long after the war, the policy toward Jewish refugees was, literally, "None is too many," my grandmother gave a detailed report of the Final Solution, condemning Western nations for their indifference:

"Asking themselves the question, 'Am I my brother's keeper?' the democratic nations of the world, our country among them, answered: 'No.'"

She ended her talk with these words: "Some action must be taken at once. If it is not, within a few months six million people will have been murdered, and the nations of the world will not be able to escape the charge of being accomplices to the bleakest crime in history."

Bub spoke English beautifully, of course. She pronounced the *h* in "white," her diction so precise that

Rose's mother, a survivor of Auschwitz, improved her newly acquired English by listening to my grandmother's broadcasts.

Writing and broadcasting were not, however, the sole domain of my grandmother's accomplishments. Bub was one of twelve women to take "M & P" — Math and Physics — at the University of Toronto, graduating with a B.A. in 1921. In 1926, pregnant with her second child, she completed the formal requirements for a Ph.D., the first woman and first Jew to receive a doctorate in physics from the university.

Naturally, whenever we had a question about homework, Bub was the person to call. It was always entertaining to watch a teacher's face while we explained that our grandmother had helped us solve a physics problem.

In our family, the desirability of a book was measured by the degree of sleep deprivation one was willing to suffer in order to reach the last page. There was no higher accolade than "I stayed up all night to finish it."

Whatever our duties, my grandmother, mother, three sisters, and I were always pining to return to our books, although it cannot be said that we read the same material. On a Bobcaygeon afternoon, I could be found on the porch, suspended in Nancy Drew's peril. My sister might be engrossed in what she called literature — a Harlequin romance. In a subsequent year, my mother is imbibing a Hebrew novel, dictionary at hand, while my grandmother sits in the rocking chair, rereading for pleasure *Black Lamb and Grey Falcon,* Rebecca West's two-volume history of the Balkans.

Perhaps my sisters and I imagined we would graduate to such maternal high-mindedness. Instead, on a dock or in bed, ignoring our importuning children, we devour mysteries to find out who did it.

For the boat trip, however, I have chosen to take out of the Toronto library the autobiography of Emily Carr, a member of the Group of Seven painters of my grandmother's era. The book meets several criteria: It is Canadian, it is about a woman artist, it is a memoir, and it is neither so compelling that I would read it instead of experiencing the moment, nor so classic that it represents aspiration rather than delight.

And yet, toward the end of the second day, I have read scarcely a page. We have been so busy, edging the boat through narrow straits, peering through the windshield for red and green buoys, tying up, setting off again. We are rubes, bumping into the walls approaching a lock, stripping the leaves from an innocent willow.

What is striking is the way my mother's family conducts itself under these trying circumstances. The lack of tension has no parallel in my childhood or even my life in New York. Like my mother, I imagine what my father, in his prime, would have done with our getting lost more than once, a barbecue that would not light, and all that slamming into other people's boats!

I have seen in myself the same hardwired impatience when life goes awry — and worked to curb it. It is a quality allied with ambition, the hunger to leave one's mark that I owe as well to my father, a majestic devotion to excellence, unforgiving of entropy in a slackening world.

Although I was raised amid a maternal clan that cultivated Jewishness as a joyful path, I am also the descendant of an illustrious rabbinic and priestly family, the Rapoports, that can trace its ancestry to the fifteenth century, among the only Jewish families with a coat of arms. I am the direct heir of one scholar, Shabbetai ha-Kohen, known as the Shakh, whose acronymic name, inscribed on my grandfather's tombstone, elicits a reverence close to awe when it is uttered among learned Jews.

My father's father, cherished eldest son, an *iluy*— child genius in Talmud — fled Russian conscription for a struggling life in Canada as a grocer and a milkman. In Poland, his sister, Tsippele, and her children have no tombstone. I picture my grandmother Nezia, for whom I am named, weeping in her Toronto kitchen in the mid-1940s when she understood with finality that her mother, my great-grandmother Sheindl, had been murdered.

Without mythologizing the past, I feel tenderly

protective of all that was desecrated and then annihilated by the Shoah. My father was born into the first generation of his family since the 1400s without a rabbi. He could not inherit from his father the intimacy with sacred texts bestowed by an intact world. That patrimony was abrogated by the shattering of the Jewish people in the twentieth century. But he did impart to me the memory of splendor that his father had conveyed to him, an oblique light of lost magnificence.

In redress, my father studied Jewish history. He was a pioneer, the first Jewish clinician in a hospital that had refused to hire even the most talented Jewish doctors before him. To his lasting regret, he did not have the ease with his people's letters and observance that my mother was given by her parents, who defied the cultural attrition surrounding them.

And so my life is fashioned by the festive round of days that is my mother's legacy, yet in the clasp of my father's birthright.

Here in the Ontario countryside, it is possible to imagine a flight from Jewish destiny. But on my tongue, the words of praise for my Creator are Hebrew, acquired through my mother, who insisted on our Jewish literacy. They arise as naturally as the concord between sky and water amid which we float at twilight.

I sit on the deck, the crickets making their summer racket beside me. The serenity of evening casts a careless grace on everything. What do I see? It is almost dark at Nassau Mills, where we are moored for the night. The trees on the shoreline facing me are black, with only a tincture of green remaining. The sky is bleached of color, pale blue above my head but fading imperceptibly to white over the woods. The lake is not transparent but a moiré of black, in which the trees are reflected, long and dusky in the rippled water.

There is a signal beauty to the end of a day on water. The Jewish calendar is lunar, and so the new day begins at dusk. Although I live in Western time, my inner life is aligned with the moon. When I walk toward home at the end of my workday, amidst men with their ties askew and women looking harried, the Jewish day is being born.

The liturgy's chants of evening and morning praise the Creator for the beauty of a renewed world. How guileless and immediate is the desire to exalt the One who made us with love as we contemplate the gorgeous gifts of creation.

When it is truly dark, Nat leads us in a procession to look at the stars. With one of the children's powerful flashlights he points out the Big Dipper, pouring invisible water over us. He shows us the W of Cassiopeia and steadies himself against a picnic table to peer through my binoculars in the hope of seeing Jupiter's moons.

The grandeur of the universe, soaring away from us in infinite solitude. The heavens, revealing God's handiwork. Walking back to the boat, Jake stays close to me; the vast darkness is so different from night in New York City. But Ella walks jauntily at the water's edge, provoked to daring by the firmament's expanse.

Both children are asleep in seconds. I watch my uncle kiss them each good night in their bunks and compose my psalm: to dwell in the house of this love forever.

And I? Awake for a second night with the child not yet born, I do not review my disappointments or anticipate sorrow. Instead, I taste these words: *peace, wonder, light, calm, peace.*

Tuesday

I N THE IVORY LIGHT OF MORNING, sky and water are one, as they were at the beginning of the world. The satin surface of the lake, unstirred by even a breath, provokes in me an immensity of memory that is almost unbearable.

There is a glory to being the first one awake, to tiptoeing from the shadowy aft of the boat onto the deck, no other living thing in sight, only the sheltering trees, sentinels against a whitened sky, echoed in water.

The wind has not yet arisen; the day is newborn. So it was on the third day of creation, the day on which

God gathered the waters, seeded the earth with fruit, and declared twice that *ki tov,* it was good.

In the shower, landscape drifting past me in the window, I quicken with recognition. I know the flickering light that splashes on the interior surfaces of the boat. I know the sight of my uncle saying his morning prayers wrapped in tallit and tefillin, as if it is natural to be the kind of person who travels the Trent-Severn Waterway with Jewish prayer accoutrements.

On the waters of Ontario we have left the city. We have also left any association with community. This is not unusual. While other families summered in Belle Ewart or Jacksons Point, my mother's family abandoned Lake Simcoe to spend fifty years in Bobcaygeon, a town where the highest number of Jewish families reached four, decades ago. Since my mother grew up in a Toronto neighborhood not only without Jews but fraught with stone-throwing Canadians, I find her family's amalgam of unparochial Judaism and Canadian noblesse oblige an intriguing puzzlement.

Whereas my father and his peers went to Harbord Collegiate, a public high school dominated by striving Jewish teenagers determined to become successful doctors and lawyers, to move away from the apartments above downtown stores and the manual labor of their parents to the leafy neighborhood of Forest Hill, my uncles went to UTS, a private high school associated with the University of Toronto that drew most of its students from the city's gentry.

My uncles, who can be found every morning (as you, half asleep, descend the stairs) draped in fringed ivory and black stripes, chanting the morning liturgy in their uniquely atonal voices, who unostentatiously murmur the long Hebrew blessings after each meal served with bread, who have among them two doctorates in physics and a stint as the deputy mayor of the city of Toronto, are heirs to this created culture.

Like so many before me, I traveled far from home. Now I dissect the legacy of my grandparents, watching Nat and my mother, querying them to extract the vitality of their inheritance.

A learned woman I know, adept in Talmud and other Jewish texts, has explained to me that some of the precepts I choose not to observe on principle must be followed nevertheless under the rubric of "the custom of the community." Such matters as clothing styles said to signify modesty or the prohibition against women conducting synagogue rites are not always determined by Jewish law per se, but are regarded as binding because the custom of the community has legal status.

My mother's family treats any new rigor in communal observance not as law but as cowardice. Always we are expected to go against the grain, to claim the temperate ground others are forsaking either from lack of desire for Jewish life, eliciting our sorrow, or because of a decision to take on more stringent practice based on norms set by younger, more ideological members of the community, eliciting our scorn.

The word for Jewish law and practice, *halakhah*, means "way." We in my mother's family have our ways. When we rent the boat, conventionally leased from Saturday to Saturday, we design our trip from Sunday to Friday. We will move through Ontario without encountering a single Jew like us. We will rejoice in the lush beauty of this province, bless the One who fashioned such a world — and return to the city in time for the Sabbath.

Occasionally I am interrogated about the legal basis for my family's less conventional religious mores. To the ill-disguised horror of some in-laws and the amusement of others, I claim to follow the Bobcaygeoner rebbe — a personage I invented to justify the ways of the clan. In a calcifying age, he is a source of increasing consolation.

For we are faithful, not only in theory but in our practice. We love the tradition into which we were born and are passionate about offering it to our children. The natural genius of my grandparents was not their commitment to Judaism, but the fusion of devotion and delight with which they transmitted it to us.

Out of loss, out of abundance, our parents taught us that the community of Israel is responsible for one another, that the Jewish homeland is a miracle, and, more rarely, that it is essential for us to be able to read our texts in their original and ancient languages.

And yet, my grandmother's birth in Toronto gave all her grandchildren an Anglo-Saxon patina that distinguished us from most of our peers at the Jewish day schools we attended. In the small Ontario towns through which we pass, we are not quite strangers. Five decades in Bobcaygeon have left their inscription.

Out of the city, I seem to have lost my capacity to hurry. By the time I finish breakfast, we have been traveling for two hours. The light has turned from gray to green. For Nat, however, there can be no sloth. By noon we must reach Peterborough, the easternmost point on our journey. Our destination is the lift lock, the great wonder of 1904 and still the highest hydraulic lift in the world.

The tranquilizing effect of the boat trip does not quite anesthetize my terror at the image of my family creaking mechanically up and up until—we are the first accident in the history of the Trent-Severn Waterway. Poor Tobi, losing his wife and current and future children in one fatal spill. I subdue my trepidation out of embarrassment.

To the exhilaration of the children, the lift lock

begins to raise our boat above the Ontario landscape. As we move effortlessly into the air, it is impossible not to be dazzled by our celestial elevation. Jake lies flat on his back to contemplate our rising. Nat kneels to pose next to Ella, his bright red windbreaker clashing spectacularly with her orange life jacket. In the photograph I take, no artifact wrought by human hands mars the immaculate emptiness beyond them.

Higher and higher, the sky endless over the earth we have temporarily abandoned. The optimism with which human beings invented such a marvel one hundred years ago seems quaint after the applications of science in our century. But it is also heartening, as if to say: Not all knowledge must mutate demonically.

When we resume our aqueous perch, the scale of the world reasserts itself. In testimony, ducks are resting on the water beside us.

Jake and Ella experiment with their snacks, tossing factory-stamped triangles and half moons onto the surface of the canal. Corn chips are especially popular; the ducks push aside one another to peck at them, bearing a hilarious resemblance to my sisters and me at a family party.

Shortly after midday, we sail into the Peterborough marina. The overnight docking fee is forty dollars, scandalizing my frugal mother and uncle. A deliberation ensues. The charge is exorbitant, although if we stay the night, we can use a neighboring hotel pool for free. The children plead their case, while my uncle and mother confer. To sleep in Peterborough will make tomorrow less leisurely, says my mother. Forty dollars is forty dollars, Nat points out, even in Canadian currency.

The Great Depression ended almost sixty years ago, but its effects are indelible. Nat and my mother were born into wealth that capsized in the crash of 1929, leaving them and their siblings to be raised in refined poverty. In my mother's family, financial caution is ingrained and lifelong.

It is the third day of the boat trip, and our tolerance of each other's idiosyncrasies is only growing. My aunt hates nature. She wants to be in a place with cafes; she is, after all these years, the girl who grew up in New York City. But I, who chose and love Manhattan, am still Canadian. Blazing across my inner eye is the summer sun of Ontario, scarce and therefore all the more desirable, the thousands of lakes in this province that are the envy of parched tropical Israel, the small towns in whose atmosphere I bask because they remind me — in their Protestant gentility or slightly rakish decline — of my family's Jewish past in Bobcaygeon.

Stay or go? The children clamor. I am a member of the generation with the longest adolescence in North American history. I am also my father's daughter. He was poor, but never doubted that he would accomplish whatever he set his mind to doing, relishing very hard work and the security he assumed would be its consequence. Nothing gave him more pleasure than treating us to ice cream, fair rides, roller skates, or any childhood pastime that signified vacation. He would laugh aloud at the sight of his daughters enjoying his beneficence.

I know in advance that the enjoyment to come is worth far more than forty dollars and, to the children's satisfaction and the relief of the others, make the executive decision: We stay. My urban aunt finds a restaurant where she can order coffee and read—her idea of a holiday—while the children are ecstatic in the hotel's pool.

I sit on the tiled ledge, remembering how I would walk with my cousins in our bathing suits and flip-flops along Front Street to the public beach in town. Thrust imposingly onto the sand was a slide we ran to climb, rungs slick from other children's wet feet, to launch ourselves, screaming, into the warm water of Sturgeon Lake.

My mother overcomes her reluctance and dons her suit. My grandmother and my mother were superb swimmers, each with a muscular crawl, whose strokes were unwavering as they met their relentless quota in lengths they counted, dock to dock, on the Bobcaygeon River. I can see Bub dipping her ankles into the gleaming shallows to accustom herself to the temperature of the water. Her skirted bathing suit flares when the river reaches her waist, and then she pushes off, white-capped head bobbing reliably as she swims toward the Boyds' dock and back to ours.

Beside me, Nat jumps in, approaching my daughter with fake menace.

"No!" Ella cries within her inflated ring, shriek accelerating as he comes nearer.

I have elected to defer reward, serving willingly as lifeguard on condition that no one rushes me when it is my turn. The anticipation of swimming without distraction endows me with limitless forbearance. I relish the sight of Jake and Ella as they frolic. Most of the rewards of parenthood are intangible: So direct a correspondence between the children's swimming lessons and their ease in water is unusually gratifying.

Everyone retires to the adjacent Jacuzzi. I turn the dial to froth, and they lie back in heat-induced stupor. I dare not go in: A prominent sign warns pregnant women against it. Instead, I must be content to swing my legs back and forth in the churning pool.

Since I was a teenager, I have associated swimming pools and bathing suits with the rebirth of my sensual self after the enforced hibernation of winter. But the glamour of near nakedness and the carnal scent of chlorine and humidity are decidedly at odds with my external identity as a pregnant mother.

Thirty years ago, my mother and I engaged in fierce battles over my first bikini and the bathing suit I bought with my grandmother's birthday money whose front and back were linked only by metal rings. From the beginning, I wanted a more stylish mother, who would ornament herself with makeup and jewelry. I can hear my mother's laugh when I proposed as a role model a neighborhood woman whose bright blue eye shadow and beehive hairdo were the epitome of chic in my six-year-old eyes.

My father is one of three brothers and my mother the sole girl among five. When my parents had four daughters within six years, they were defenseless. As we became teenagers, our uncle Rafe was the only one in the extended family who could affirm our womanness alongside our wit. His nieces reveled in his appreciation, which had no trace of prurience and was not, in any case, expressed in words, but in the tacit exchanges that were the currency of his love.

My mother was at a loss when confronted with a daughter whose desire to flaunt her long-awaited woman's body was so alien, so alarming. Now our friction over pleasure is limited to her half-hearted objections to my indulgence in rich desserts. The chasm between the generations has narrowed to a debate about food.

She is sixty-nine and I am forty-four. Soon, I tell

her, we will be the same age. Still antithetical in temperament, we are increasingly compatible.

In the households of my friends and in ours when I was young, fathers left for work and returned "beat," retreating to their bedrooms to change out of their suits, to their dens to "unwind" in front of the television, to dinner and pre-bedtime naps that overtook them on the living room couch. Even executive fathers were home each night by six, although often they ate alone, too depleted by running the world to contend with their rowdy children.

Not one of the mothers I knew worked outside the house, unless they were survivors of the Shoah who helped their husbands in the store — and then only until they could afford to stay home.

At twenty-four, my mother left graduate school — in education, of course — to be married. My second sister married before her twenty-fourth birthday, but the rest of us are women of our time. I was thirty-two, and my third and fourth sisters were older. And yet I came of age in a world where it was considered necessary to hold an earnest conversation in Home Economics about the problem of being a girl who is smarter than her boyfriend. (The answer was never: Dump the boyfriend.)

Although my cousins, my sisters, and I spoke constantly of our grandmother's distinction, we did not say to ourselves then: Our mothers work in the home, but our grandmother had five children, earned a Ph.D. in physics, wrote her columns, broadcast on the radio for decades, and founded a school. She represented in her person more choices than we saw around us in the sum of women we knew when we were girls. Even today, an era of unprecedented accomplishment by women, she is unique in what she undertook, in how she fashioned her life.

Only now that we have children of our own have we returned to marvel at my mother. As teenage feminists, we used to tell her to get a real job; these days we call to ask her how on earth she managed. How did you buy the winter coats, write the school notes, help patiently with homework, enroll us in piano lessons, drive us to ice skating, make thousands of meals without praise or public esteem for the unrelenting labor of motherhood?

My mother relishes our contrition. Ahead of me, she has become my teacher.

In my bathing suit, I am in the indeterminate stage of pregnancy I remember, my waistline not yet sufficiently distended for an onlooker to be certain enough to congratulate me. The maintenance of an urban body, that incessant project of adult life, is taxing. But on the boat trip, my stomach need not be constrained for the sleek veneer of work. I am, instead, thankfully at ease in oversize T-shirts and leggings. Soon enough, I will be returned to my calculations of whether I can have chocolate once a day without betraying my vanity. Here, the relinquishment of my waist is a startling liberation from the upkeep of a willowy silhouette.

Although pregnancy is the stamp of sex, my baggy clothes have rendered me curiously neutral, not only to others but to myself. Everyone who travels by boat is dressed in loose, practical clothes that hang away from the body. And perhaps because I am in the company of my uncle, aunt, and mother, or because of the children, I feel childlike, too, suspended between old and young without commitment.

Dressed and glowing after our swim, we sally back to the boat. My mother and aunt prepare fresh corn. Nat reads the *Globe and Mail,* enjoying idleness at last. Ora believes in ignoring the news, especially on vacation, but my mother, uncle, and I are addicted, as my grandmother was. On summer mornings in Bobcaygeon I would walk at her side, hurrying slightly to keep up with her, to the barbershop on Bolton Street where she had a standing order for the *Globe.*

I sit beside my uncle to write in my journal, snared by the writer's dilemma: I can either record life faithfully or live it.

At the table my uncle and my mother discuss which of their grandparents was the most fun. Although their mother's family was extroverted compared to the straitlaced relatives on their father's side, their paternal grandfather wins nevertheless.

Their choice is bolstered when I play the game their father played with me, which is my only recollection of him. I put my hand on Ella's stomach and "see" each item of her dinner. My mother says, "Dad learned that game from *his* father." The pedigree of memory.

We stroll into town for ice cream. Even my mother, after looking in vain for frozen yogurt, lets down her cholesterol guard. While I return to the boat with the children, my mother and uncle go off together. I watch them from behind, their wiry frames and upright posture identical and poignant. I imagine they are talking about illness and affliction, those family circumstances that cannot be negotiated. My mother is private, and my uncle a trustworthy confidant.

The marina is nearly empty. A faint sense of hazard, the small-town idleness of lurking teenagers, accompanies us back to the boat. But the evening sky is electric, casting the remains of gold light in small patches on the navy blue water and then exploding into a flamboyant sunset in the far west.

I read the children a chapter in the adventures of the Hardy Boys. They doze off, but I cannot sleep until I hear the latch of the screen door, signifying the return of my mother—a reversal of the many times I tormented her by staying out all night, believing I was immortal.

Asleep by ten, I wake at one, alert. In my mind are the pansies, impatiens, and geraniums I saw today at the marina. As a child in Bobcaygeon I would pass those flowers, spilling in tidy profusion over the beds of Mrs. Boyd's front garden when I walked into town with my grandmother. Sometimes I knelt before the pansies, entranced by the velvety petals, purple deepening to the evocative black that demanded the stroke of a finger, eliciting Bub's remonstrance.

Among the flares that light my life is the fact that we gave our daughter my grandmother's name. Although the flutter of saying it aloud subsided after her infancy, it has been renewed as we approach Bobcaygeon. Every time I call Ella in the presence of my mother and uncle, I feel I am bringing my grandmother back to life. Ella will be shaped by her story—and my grandmother was not an ordinary person.

Today, however, Ora described a walk she took with my grandmother twenty years ago, during which Bub asked her suddenly, "Do you think I should get a facelift?"

My cerebral grandmother! My aunt added, "I was in my forties, and I couldn't imagine what my wrinkles would seem like in my seventies."

Now I am in my forties.

"Do you know," my aunt continued, "that there were women in the family jealous of your mother because she has so few wrinkles?"

In the past, my mother's humility deterred our compliments. But watching her dart about the boat or play tag with my children, I notice her sensational youthfulness as if for the first time.

When I was growing up, my mother's prudence was inhibiting. On this journey, however, seeing her mouth on her brother's face and, movingly, on my daughter's, I feel my body composed in harmony with hers.

Around three, all the adults wake. I whisper, "Mom," as she comes into the galley facing my bed. She sits down beside me to stroke my hand.

"Is this soothing or annoying?" she asks in her unassuming way.

"Soothing," I say.

She kisses me on the cheek and says, "Is it nice to be kissed good night by your Mummy?"

"Yes," I tell her. But the tears came well before she asked.

Wednesday

A GRAY DAY OVER GRAY WATER, reflecting my weariness. We have passed the midpoint of the boat trip. Instead of our waking each day to a new world, we will reverse lock numbers and names, returning through Lake Buckhorn to Pigeon Lake, where we began. And then farther west.

Shuffling from my tousled sleeping bag onto the deck, I succumb to the forlorn quality of the light. There is no journey without at least one such day, when the soul quails before a resurgence of troubles abounding. Each of us is in a private realm this morning. We do not speak of Bobcaygeon. Perhaps because the object of our journey lies before us, we are cautious. Even before we reach the town, we are saying good-bye.

As we pass through Nassau Mills, Jake tells the lock mistress, "We meet again."

"See you later," she replies.

"Not likely," says my uncle.

"Don't say that," I say childishly. "We have to come back."

"Of course we will," he assures me.

But when I calculate, I see that by the time the baby is five, Nat will be closer to eighty than to seventy. I try to quell a familiar terror, of loss, of endings.

There is an art to saying good-bye and a paradox. My uncle Rafe taught me both when we said good-bye to Bobcaygeon. Only if you acknowledge parting, embrace it without flinching, can you leave well. If you deny its imminence, the agony of farewell is never subdued, tainting the present because it was withheld.

And so when my grandmother was almost eighty, when the shadow of the concrete bridge cast itself over the dock, and the powers that be (those mysterious forces) threatened to expand the road into a highway, the cottage was sold.

At the end of the summer of 1975, Rafe and I drove to Bobcaygeon for the last time. I was then a person so afraid of endings that I had never willfully left anyone or anything. But Rafe decreed the day a celebration, a festival from which all sadness was banished. We took pictures everywhere, beneath the sign that said "Front Street," on the dining room window seat from which as children we jumped onto the porch bed, in the claw-footed bathtub, and on the dock as I lay in my bathing suit, amazed by how much more experience I had in love.

All day we laughed in air green as grass. We invented a song about the cottage to the tune of "Mairzy Doates" that the family sings to this day. We bought Bob-caygeon T-shirts so ugly they were cool and preened in them before my somewhat nonplussed grandmother. And I, twenty-two years old and believing there was nothing about the heart left for me to learn, saw that the more con-scious we were of parting, the more reconciled we became.

The lesson did not keep. I could not decide to ini-tiate the finale of romance until it was far past time or until the other did the deed for both of us, leaving me unsuit-ably grief-stricken, considering I had secretly longed for such an eventuality. I preferred to be left, with all its attending anguish, than to admit the dilution of love.

Still, I did not forget the day of farewell to Bob-caygeon, which Rafe and I cited with surprising frequency. Because of the way we said good-bye, the deliberateness, the decision to commemorate, there was none of the bitter aftertaste when something momentous has been left undone.

I could return to Bobcaygeon any time I chose. When I lay sleepless on business trips, the cottage, the road, the walk into town would appear, as if they were still in the future. What was it, I would conjecture with Rafe, about a down-at-heels old cottage in Ontario that continued to enchant us? He could not put it into words but offered his sweet smile of empathy.

Throughout these days I have been determined not to imagine, not to foresee. As in the liturgy of Passover, I bargain: To have embarked on the boat trip would be enough. To have seen the lakes again would be enough.

Secretly, of course, I want everything, as I always have. My restraint is a conceit of middle age, to which I submit only because life has taught me, a most recalcitrant student, that I must. True, in the face of illness and death, ordinary life has a beauty I could never have coveted in my twenties, when I yearned for an existence based solely on poetry. And yet I must be careful. My cousins have warned me that the town is unrecognizable. The bridge over the river that prompted my grandmother to sell the house is hideous. The cottage was razed; the house built on the plot bears no resemblance to ours, they say. Above all, I fear that tomorrow will be a somber day, bleak, resisting memory.

Despite my trepidation, the weather has been fair. Even inauspicious mornings have been heartened by a noon sun. Never sweltering or oppressive, the air has retained its autumnal cast, contributing a satisfying inflection of melancholy to perfection. For the journey has been perfect, as if I have distilled all my summers into an essence and swallowed it whole.

The power of the boat trip has been generated by dailiness, the modest discoveries that become so resonant in the presence of my family. And yes, they have been sufficient. In fact, the sustenance of each day's unfolding has been the most important of the journey's gifts. The trip is a meditation, not a narrative. A falsely imposed climax will lead to disappointment, I tell myself, wishing tomorrow to come upon me almost by accident.

But my fatigue, compounded by nights of wakefulness, can no longer be offset by caffeine or catnaps. I have entered the state of weariness I remember from my adolescence, my serenity infiltrated by existential worry—the baby's health, my dreams as a writer, my limitations as a human being. My mind flits among unanswerable questions: How, with a new baby, will I earn a living and continue to write? Will Tobi and I live to see our third child grown? What will happen to my parents as my father's memory diminishes?

I reason with myself sternly, but I cannot extricate myself from the bonds of fear. When I walk onto the deck, the moisture-laden wind twists my hair into a mad corona.

I sense rather than see a presence beside me. It is Ella, laughing at my coiffure. Her uncensored joy, the boat's rocking, the tang of air over water begin their invigorating magic. It is impossible to remain mired in dour speculation.

Strangely, as we travel back, the lockmasters seem to be waiting for us. Now we discover that when marine traffic is light, they telephone ahead to prepare their counterparts for boats to come.

By Lock 23, we are bantering with the lockmaster, whose brown shorts and matching pinstriped shirt give him the appearance of a souvenir mascot.

No doubt, we say, someone called to warn him that the worst sailors on the Trent Canal system are approaching.

"You're not nearly the worst boat I've seen," he tells us cheerfully.

Of course we must hear his story.

"A guy came in, full throttle," the man begins his tale with gusto. "We knew he wouldn't stop; he was a show-off we'd met before. Sure enough, he crashed into the gate. His windshield blew out, and his barbecue went into the drink."

We are memorizing the phrase "into the drink."

"So his girlfriend panicked," our narrator contin-ues. "She ran through the boat to the back deck and slipped on the indoor/outdoor carpeting. Her bathing suit bottom came right off. Was her ass red!"

The children are agog. They refer to the story throughout the morning, sanctioned by the fact that an official Canadian park ranger has used forbidden language without compunction.

By lunchtime, however, Jake and Ella are stir-crazy. My mother volunteers to read to them. Sitting on the front deck, the canal widening, breathtakingly, into an Ontario lake, they listen to her recount the next feat of the imperishable Hardy Boys, my daughter absorbed, my son riveted. So my mother would read to me, and her mother to her. This is the legacy of my family — not gold or jewels but a passion for the written word.

I put down my journal to savor the sight.

Among other enlightenments, the boat trip is a paean to the ability of humankind to keep learning. We are no longer amateurs. Four days after we launched our-selves onto the lakes of Ontario, we have mastered the tricks of this houseboat, overcorrecting as we negotiate the buoys, cutting the motor at the precise moment that allows us to enter the lock without a scratch.

On our left as we proceed is a crowded summer resort, small houses clustered together.

"Looks like a *kochalein* community," my uncle exclaims to my mother. They both smile.

I smile, too, because I never hear either of them speak a word of Yiddish. My grandmother, born in Canada, spoke the King's English. My mother placed her bets on Hebrew as the language of the Jews. Although my father, son of immigrants, knew Yiddish as his first language, my mother picked up scraps of it only because she had studied German.

My sisters and I know Hebrew and no Yiddish at all, not even enough to understand the punch lines of jokes that are clearly uproarious.

Thus my bemusement at my uncle's use of a Yiddish term that I presume means some version of "bungalow colony." There is something delicious about his juxtaposition of a Catskills image on upright Ontario. The sight also inspires Nat to go swimming in the middle of the lake, his archetype of summer leisure.

We lower the anchor; he descends the truncated ladder at the back of the boat and briskly begins.

"Is it cold?" I naturally ask him.

"It's wonderful," he emphasizes.

But when it is time for him to get out, he cannot get a purchase on the too-short and slippery metal ladder. Its square rungs cut into his palms and cause him to fall back into the water.

For the first few minutes, we find it funny, and then we grow alarmed. The water is frigid, it is late in the afternoon, there is no boat in sight to which we can appeal, and my uncle is not young. How, in fact, will he get out?

Suddenly I remember the way we swam against the thrust of the Bobcaygeon River for the beatitude of an effortless return. Beneath the high sun and the gorgeous trees was a frisson of danger: If we lay on our backs, carried by the river's velocity from Mrs. Boyd's dock to ours, but missed the right second to grasp the rungs of our dock's ladder, we might be swept out to sea! For shortly past our cottage the river opened to meet the lake, which we could see from our dock's safety, a vast expanse of water without shore.

My uncle is not panicking, but even with the human chain we form, we are unable to lift him.

"Adventure, adventure," my mother says, trying to dispel the anxiety on Jake's face.

"I'm sick of adventure," says my urban son. He has readied an adult-size life jacket, just in case.

I am wavering between confidence that we will contrive a solution to this dilemma and primitive dread.

We pull again. Nat slips from our grasp. We regroup — and still he falls back.

Anxiety triumphs. The shadows of the trees lengthen over the water, and I give way to despair.

Finally, through an inspired combination of the life buoy, our hauling, and his exertion, Nat climbs triumphantly onto the deck.

The brush with uncertainty has debilitated me. While my mother teaches my children the game in which they take turns making pencil lines until they form closed boxes, I fall into relieved sleep. In New York I do not nap, but on the boat trip I take shameful pleasure in the knowledge that my condition will be indulged.

Time passes. When I open my eyes, we are gliding due west between islands of pine, the boat's path lit by a ship's hull of glossy yellow, leaving a radiant wake before us. The children are rambunctious, the wind is up, and because of our small adventure we will not reach Buckhorn as planned. Instead, we moor at Lovesick, the most isolated of our overnight settings.

Jake is disappointed. He will not be able to buy the artificial bait that is his newest souvenir obsession. My aunt bemoans the lack of cafes. Lovesick is too rural for her taste. My own sobriety is laced with a consciousness of endings. Today has been a less lyrical day. I tell myself not every day can be revelatory. For a woman of my ardor, the acknowledgment is a concession. I cannot tell if I am acquiring wisdom or admitting defeat.

We tie up in cloudy coolness, but then, surprisingly, the evening grows clear and clearer still. A pink sunset washes the sky and water with color as artificial as cotton candy. Suddenly, as I emerge from the lock's bathroom, there is a downpour. I watch the sheets of rain with resignation.

Below me, as I wait, my mother stands in her dark green slicker, vigilant over the barbecue.

When the torrent abates, I sprint for the boat.

"Perhaps," my uncle speculates, "there will be a rainbow."

I cannot remember the last time I saw one.

My uncle moves down the pier. "You might do better here," he says allusively.

Behind the trees, in a gossamer arc, a rainbow adorns the sky. And then a double rainbow, one arc above the other in the gloaming.

At the end of the biblical flood tale, a rainbow is the sign of the covenant between God and humanity that such destruction will not be wreaked upon us again. I long for the blessing upon seeing a rainbow, whose syllables I cannot quite retrieve.

Nat goes inside for his prayer book to find the Hebrew words for me. Everyone wants to say them aloud, a staggered chorus of praise.

"Great special effect," I say to my uncle, hugging him. "Thanks for planning it."

He smiles like a little boy. And then my mother

speaks before the darkening galley window with uncustomary yearning. "I wish I could bottle this," she tells me as I stand close to her. "But no matter how hard you try to hold onto it, you can't."

I know.

All my life, my grandmother was the spine of the family, stalwart, never ill, her threshold of pain so high that we never heard her complain.

Whenever I came back to Toronto, she was there. We spoke of books, of writing and the Jews, and occasionally of politics. In later years she could not walk with ease, relinquishing the miles she used to stride well after her peers had surrendered to a more typical old age. She was sometimes bored, she said, her eyes not able to read for the long stretches to which she was accustomed. But grandchildren and their children dropped by. Her cinnamon buns were waiting in the freezer to be warmed. She relished our stories and accomplishments, still exacting, withholding comment, an occasional acerbic judgment escaping to remind us that her wit and aphorisms were readily at hand, her extraordinary mind undimmed.

When my mother called, then, to say that Bub was in the hospital, taken on Shabbat, her breath short, her lungs filling, I asked if I should come. "She's stable," said my mother in the family's low-key way. "I don't think it's necessary."

I forgot that my mother, like her mother, thinks most things are not necessary. I could hear Bub's uttering her hallmark phrase, "Don't make a fuss." I did not go. I called my mother frequently but did not call my grandmother, knowing that everyone was there, in and out of her room, subliminally expecting that any day now she would be home, where I could speak to her just as well, as she would say.

By Tuesday she was not conscious of where she was. That night, unaware, I met two friends for dinner. On our way to a class, I lumbered into a cab with several packages and reached for my purse to be sure I could pay the fare.

My purse was gone. Panic-stricken, I dashed out of the cab, waving the driver on, to search the restaurant. We had been sitting at the back, and I had left seconds ago, but my query drew a blank face from the manager. As he conscientiously helped me look, inviting me to check the storage cupboards, I suspected his complicity but could prove nothing.

Everything was in that bag. My house keys, my ID, gift certificates I foolishly carried in case I passed the appropriate store. Instead of going to the class, I borrowed a quarter and called home to tell Tobi we would have to replace the locks, tonight.

"I have sad news," he said.

"Bub," I answered immediately.

He confirmed it. When I began to sob, my friends thought I was overcome by the loss of my bag.

The rest of the night was a confusion of locksmith, reservations, and telephone plans, my pocketbook conflated forever with my grandmother — irretrievable. To this day, I see Bub in the world to come, my purse in her hand.

So ashamed was I of my dereliction in not calling her that I could not bear to mention it to my mother.

Later she told me of her own remorse, she who had visited Bub every day, picked up groceries or prescriptions, driven her wherever she had to go.

"I never held her hand on the last day of her life," my mother said. "If only I had known."

"Mom, you couldn't have been a better daughter."

She demurred. And then she quoted Bub's brother, a scholar and Army chaplain, who spoke this truth: "No matter how much you do, you never feel it was enough."

My grandmother would be astonished to learn that I think about her every day. Once, leaving Boston at the end of a business trip, I took a detour to see an exhibition of Monet's late paintings. There was the bridge at Giverny, at dawn and at dusk, in desperation and thanksgiving, constant only in its allure for Monet, who never tired of rendering its guises.

So I justify to myself the sway of my grand-mother over me. Unbidden, she appears in my writing with increasing frequency. So diffident she could not abide praise — if I told her I missed her when I called from New York, she said, "No, you don't" — she would be mortified by such a public acknowledgment of my de-votion. I find this recognition a perversely satisfying rec-ompense for her leaving me.

For my uncle, my mother, and me, the boat trip is a communion with her memory. We look up at the Ontario sky with the same awe we felt when we walked with her as she taught us the constellations.

The stars at Lovesick are sensational. My daugh-ter and I venture into the dark to see them, and then my mother joins us silently.

As I zip myself into my sleeping bag, other im-ages of the day appear: the children calling out "red light, green light" to my mother, the colors of their anoraks unusually vivid in the gathering dusk. My uncle reciting the games they played for hours on drowsy Bobcaygeon afternoons — Anagrams, Monopoly, Hearts. The children fishing at twilight with a white-blond local girl called Brandi.

Even as I try to lull my mind into satiety, my body mutinies. Everyone has fallen asleep, but my blood beats as if it were bright day. I place a finger at the base of my throat and try to mesh my breathing with the rhythm of the water, lapping in the window beside me like the river when I slept on the porch bed at the cottage.

At midnight, the possibility of rest tantalizes and eludes me. It is preposterous to try to seduce Morpheus with images of childhood summers. Ordinariness has fled: I cannot pretend that dawn will inaugurate a day like any other.

Within hours, we will sail into Bobcaygeon.

Thursday

NEARLY THIRTY YEARS AGO, when I lay on the dock in Sabbath peace, dreaming of love, I could not know that so soon I would be drowning in its honeyed density. To contemplate that summer of waiting, to remember the mercy afforded me by Bobcaygeon, time suspended in reverie, anointing the quotidian as I basked in my grandmother's tranquility, my younger cousins' play, harmony undarkened by desire, and now to think: Today.

What do I want? What will complete the quest? Not to return to then, to the random lurch of exultation and despondency. Not to before: before the tempering gifts of work and vocation, of husband and children. But to be privileged to taste once more the heady potion of yearning and splendor.

If I can be granted the uncut opium, pure memory, released into the coming days, infusing the winter with summer's eternity, I will be able, at the close of this journey, to reenter the life I have chosen—the coming child, the urban clang, the surging uncertainties, the black and white of youth not only moderated but sullied at times by compromise—to inhabit, each day, the benediction of the past.

Not that on this morning I am dewy with the light of a generous past. No, I am bone weary, spent, the customary state of a working mother with young children. The boat trip has already bestowed a surfeit of unanticipated gifts, but my physical well-being is not among them.

Hoping that exercise will offset my depleted state, I walk briskly up and down the pier, resigned to fatigue and bemused. Before a long-awaited reunion, I am not the kind to drift into pacific sleep in order to be rested for the morrow. Sedate preparation has never been my habit.

On the narrow cement path that flanks the water, I pass my mother. She, too, is walking purposefully. From whom, after all, did I learn to leaven sloth with exercise? As she passes me in turn, she says, "It's so gorgeous I could cry."

I have studied my parents with fascination as they get older, as if they were sacred texts I might decode. As I struggle to dilute my intensity, my mother's neutral disposition is increasingly potent with feeling.

At the breakfast table she says again, "If only you could bottle it. But it fades away, barely a memory."

I do not mourn. For me, memory is tangible, always present. My recollections are objects, available to scrutinize, to savor, even to alter. Although swaths of time at work or in love cannot be redeemed, I can, if I choose, enter moments of such rapture that their chronological duration bears no relationship to the precision with which I can recall each detail.

Even before we reach Bobcaygeon, I know that the boat trip will constitute such a memory. I will be dwelling within it for the rest of my days, returning as I have to Bobcaygeon, almost a quarter of a century — I recite to myself — after I walked down Front Street to the cottage for the last time.

This ability to regain the past as if it were present is not nostalgia. I do not want to live then; I ask that then be now, that I can at will plunge into time, those moments when — through devotion, or even pain — we are granted a taste of immortality. Such a re-creation has been the promise of this journey.

When I was sixteen, Bobcaygeon was an overture. Like pregnancy, for at the beginning of each child, my expanding body reverses its overt sexual kindling. All the years of thinness and withholding, of designing my body to please men, or my idea of them, and then, as a consequence of sex, I grow round, losing first the curve from waist to hip that externalizes the contemporary woman's restraint for the sake of enticement.

Throughout the summer, as I went about my life in New York, I was alert to my body's new and secret status, from the moment I woke until, in sleep, I lost consciousness. And sometimes, even in sleep, as I dreamed. But on the boat trip I find myself forgetting that I'm pregnant, as if I had invented the idea, put it forth among my closest friends, and then changed my mind. To travel to Bobcaygeon, then, is metaphorically apt, for I am returning to the summer before I so willingly exchanged the longing for something to happen for the ardor and anguish when it did.

Today, thankfully, I do not have to endure the unbearable waiting that is intrinsic to passion. The nature of the encounter I will have on this very day depends upon my imagination. Will it fail me, by conjuring an expectation that cannot be met, because it relies on chance — light, weather, the patience of my children? My prayer is modest: Let me be alive now as well as then, a palimpsest, without barrier or intermediary.

As if we were beginning again, we travel through Buckhorn, the first lock of our trip five days ago, toward Pigeon Lake.

I honor the day by taking a shower, dousing myself in heated water as the lake fills the window. When I listen to the words I am singing, I have chosen "The Dawntreader," a song from Joni Mitchell's first album about leaving the city for the sea.

Revived, I am suffused with summer, but the weather is gray. My uncle gently teases me: I will not see the gold light we remember.

Throughout my life I have alternated grandiose hope with irrefutable despair, but today my uncle's placid and familiar pessimism only reinforces my adamance. Although the sky augurs rain, I am confident. I have tried to adopt my maternal lineage's acceptance of what cannot be changed — the weather being a paradigmatic example — but on this day I reject the mode of courtly resignation. Defying Nat's skepticism, I declare that it will be a beautiful day.

The laminated book of navigation maps is draped over the coffee table. My finger traces our route, lingering over the names as if they were in Braille and could signify through a single layer of my skin the momentousness of our passage. Today, soon, less than an hour, is my chant.

As we glide north on Pigeon Lake, my uncle begins to recant. Shortly after noon, the sky has brightened, the sun almost piercing the opaque dome over us. I do not want to live symbolically, as I did in my youth, flayed by the vagaries of my interior world. But there is no mistaking the turn of the day.

We leave the lake for the river.

Fatigue has fled. We are all mindful now — Nat and my mother, who knew the town through decades of their lives; Ora, for our sake; and Jake and Ella, who have never been here but intuit our awakening.

The extravagant trees bend over the narrowing water. A development of summer condos, new to us. Time quickens.

Look. The green boathouse.

There. The dock.

Ahead. The pale lawn.

As I distinguish them, they are already behind me. I scarcely tell myself the name of one when the next appears and dissolves. In the photographs I take, the images will seem far more defined and distant than the immediacy of this dreamy world, so close we can almost reach over the railing of the deck to touch it.

Despite the massive bridge, the setting of the cottage at the curve of the river is ravishing. A surge of jubilation charges every cell as my body affirms the quintessence of this place.

We enter Bobcaygeon as in a magician's tale, floating past Gordon's marina into the heart of town to dock at the foot of the library. The sun is lavish, the air suddenly so hot that I begin to take off layers of clothing as we tie up. I knot my sweatshirt around my waist and then, despising my conservatism, fling it recklessly into the depths of the boat. In ritual procession, we mount the grassy bank to the road.

My uncle, my mother, and I were bewitched by the library, which held in its collection all the books that the library in the city was too effete to carry. If you took out a book you longed to read, you were permitted to return it the following summer, a privilege I found intoxicating. The endless span of time — from the laden air of July through the darkening fall and the drab monotony of Toronto's winter, round into spring at last, the fluted daffodils, and the hint of long-anticipated summer — was condensed by the implicit confidence of the library: We, its seasonal patrons, shall return.

After twenty years, we have. A little shyly, as if into a sanctuary, we enter. Jake immediately finds the Hardy Boys' adventures. We take a picture of him, volume in hand. Then, in an alcove, I pose with a Nancy Drew book. My uncle and mother stand beneath a sign that dedicates the room to Amy Cosh, the librarian they knew as children.

The library is strangely bright. Perhaps it is the new wallpaper that has routed the hushed languor of our memories. The front room, where books are checked out, is more atmospheric. We introduce ourselves to the two librarians behind the desk. The scent of their face powder and their softly sculpted hair evoke my grandmother. I want souvenirs; the librarians apologize for the photo-copied bookmarks, all they have.

Instantly I embark on a fantasy of astonishing literary success, when I return to Bobcaygeon to endow the library with an infinite supply of elegant bookmarks. They will be in honor of my grandmother, of course, and the fifty years my family contributed to the summer life of the town. With nothing else to memorialize us, the imaginary bookmarks would also remind every upstanding denizen that four generations of an observant Jewish family had been neighbors.

I look up. Near the ceiling are two shelves of old leather volumes, titles stamped in gilt. They are seldom lent, the librarians say. Instead, they rest in Olympian silence, testifying to the days of my grandmother's youth, of Shakespeare read aloud from books like these. Relics, they are nonetheless comforting.

My mother and uncle reminisce with the librarians about Miss Cosh while I buy up packets of note cards that bear a sketch of the building. Already I know I will never use them.

By the time we leave, the day has become the one I pictured, ablaze with August sun. We must hurry to Front Street, I tell the others. I cannot lose this light before we reach the place where the cottage stood.

The children, however, are nine and five years old. They will not be able to walk farther without sustenance. Their legs give way easily, and I am prudent enough to know how I will feel about their dawdling. We turn down Bolton Street and there, before my eyes, is the IGA, un-altered, as if it were decades ago and I am entering the store with my grandmother to buy Coke and Alpha-Bits and all the food our parents have banned that she miracu-lously allows.

Jake and Ella race down the aisles, choosing their favorite chocolate bars and looking for orange juice in con-centrate, which they claim tastes better than pure juice. Ready at last, they insist that I carry their clumsy provisions. The bottles bump my calf rhythmically as we set out.

We pass the old post office, deserted and dere-lict. This abandoned building was a bustling destination for my grandmother and me, as I accompanied her in our stroll from the cottage to get the mail. I would stand on tiptoe to inquire of the postmistress for letters under *R*, the initial of my mother's family name. The romance of asking for mail and receiving a packet.

"Remember the three bridges?" says my uncle.

Bobcaygeon is set at the picturesque intersection of a river and two lakes. Always, there is water to rest the eye—the river before the cottage, the lake on the other side of the bridge, the canal.

We cross the second bridge and another, until we are at the start of Front Street.

"There was the movie theater," Nat says to my mother, pointing across the street to no place. She walks over to look at the stone trough from which horses used to drink. At the Front Street sign, we replicate the photograph I took with Rafe on the day we said good-bye.

Facing us is Locust Lodge, now the Bobcaygeon Inn and Spa. I try to imagine a stay at the spa, but fail. I cannot translate into commerce the repose of memory.

Down the road is a white building that was once Edgar's. It is wrecked and in the process of being demolished. I can re-create the delight of shivering in shorts during the brief arctic when Mrs. Edgar pulled open the heavy freezer door so that we could retrieve a brisket to prepare for the Sabbath.

Despite its pretty setting along the river, Front Street is shabby, with hardscrabble lots and a bed-and-breakfast advertising available rooms. Was it always this way? Am I one of multitudes who return after a long absence to a childhood place that now seems diminished?

Disappointment is one emotion I will not allow. I suspend desire.

"Wasn't there a spot near here," I ask my uncle, "where people could back their boats from the road right onto the water?"

No one remembers. As I am half doubting myself, wondering if the road has been repaved or even if I invented it, the place manifests itself before my eyes. Here, to my fascination, cars would reverse, blocking the road, to slip their attached boats onto the river.

I cannot express to the others the sensation of reencountering it. The sight of the paved drive sloping into the river, without transition or warning, generates in me the same odd surprise I felt as a child. The immediate juxtaposition of land and water still makes my breath catch. In the story of the world's beginning, God's first deed after the creation of light is the recovery and distinction of firmament from water.

I am here not to be born but to be reborn. Lord, I pray, let me taste even the smallest measure.

My mother and uncle are far ahead, talking intently. "Wait up," I call out to them in the locution of childhood. I do not want to miss a word of the stories they are telling each other about the old days. But they do not hear me. Something in me recognizes that their sibling symmetry should be inviolate. I do not belong with them, hungry as I am to listen to their exchanges. Jake and Ella, in the company of my aunt, move forward more aimlessly. I am last. Inevitably, it is right for me to be alone.

Until now, I have been fixed in the present, ambling toward the cottage site on a pleasant, slightly overheated summer day. The road narrows and jogs a bit, overhung with the opulent green of trees at their peak. I take a breath of the still air.

The perfume of all summers, of vegetation almost too ripe, of sun and water, gravel, trees, and sky. Everything, this day and the past that led up to it, dissolves. Sauntering down Front Street, alongside the leafy glory of Bobcaygeon's century-old trees and the gleam of river among their branches, like the willows draping the river as we sailed in, I have my Proustian moment. It is this scent that remains, evergreen, unassailable by time, by speculators, by the destruction of the cottage — even by death.

As I bear within my aging body a new life, so this fragrance of time distilled, captured in a single breath, will assume the task of memory.

Long ago, I described to an older friend the burden of my consciousness, its relentless translation of experience into language that prevented me from sleeping and was a barricade against living. "If this is how I am now," I said, "think how much worse I'll be when I'm old."

He looked at me sagely. "When you're old," he said, "and you cannot rely on your physical capacities, you will have a rich inner life for sustenance."

All journeys are inward now. My return to Bobcaygeon is not a six-day trip to a once familiar place. It is the assent of a benign universe, saying to me: Nothing was in vain. Nothing is lost.

When you are young, pain is not only consuming but without end. You pray that you will not have to live in such an exposed state, as if your skin is abraded every day by waking up.

Then, over time, you learn resistance, more and more rapidly, until the suffering of youth is bemusing and you thank the Almighty that you do not have to relive those years.

But if in your forties you reencounter the might, the dominion of emotion, and if you are honest, the story is no longer as simple as it seemed. You are, it must be confessed, in awe of feeling's resplendence, its omnipotence, like a wonder of nature to which people flock, their faces rapt, the water endlessly falling, stronger than death.

Of course, I am greedy for eternity, like any

romantic. I want to reap the most wanton harvest pain-lessly, to be restored to the purity of youthful desire — but with all the wisdom earned until today.

My mother and uncle ahead, the children before me on the road, I pass Mrs. Boyd's cottage. The house looks fit, but less bedecked in marigolds and pansies than I recall. I peer around the back, feeling illicit. There is the flourish of bright flowers to match my memory.

Now I walk toward where the cottage was, hoping that the empty lot beside the house is still there. On the field, when I was six, we played horseshoes, a game I have not played since, although I can feel against my palm the weight of warm metal and hear the clang when I managed to sling the shoe around the stake poking above the weeds.

The lot, however, has been domesticated by a tidy, blunt triplex, the one-story building trimmed in red and white that has replaced my grandmother's house. On the porch sits the very woman who bought it. Nat recognizes her from the first boat trip a decade ago. Her husband is beside her, a television in the background, framed by the open door. Behind us, the concrete bridge dominates the water.

My mother, introducing herself, chats with the owner eagerly.

"Oh, yes," the woman replies, "we've had others from your family come from time to time."

I smile when I consider the pilgrimage. The triplex is no Jerusalem, but the place is numinous for all of us.

Ora, the children, and I wait at the top of the stairs leading to the dock. After a decent interval, I slip down the first stone slabs. Now the others are above me on the small, grassy patch beside the gravel rectangle where we would park the car, flinging open the door to hug my grandmother, who stood vigil until our safe arrival.

I stand on the dock from which my uncle would leap into the river with a yowl of anticipatory pleasure, drowning any residue of his hot drive from Toronto. On the rocks beside me, my grandmother entered the water to swim in even strokes to Mrs. Boyd's cottage and back. Here I lay in my newly acquired bikini on a body that could finally sport it, daydreaming about a future that would take me far from Toronto to vistas and experiences I could not even name, to emotions I recognized only from books.

Turning my back to the bridge, the lawn across the river still verdant but without the house whose windows once glinted like diamonds, the girl I was and the weekends that saved me are so palpable that I can feel the sun-warmed wood beneath my tanning limbs, hear my grandmother calling us through the screen door to Shabbat lunch.

It is incomprehensible that my uncles are in their sixties and seventies, that my grandmother is gone and I am not a teenager but a forty-four-year-old woman. And yet so much of what I wanted has transpired. All the intensity of love I could have desired, and the pain that was its familiar, the despair and bliss of writing, of earning my livelihood, the sanctuary of marriage, of children, the urbanity, the glamour — all granted to me. My life has been replete, encompassing the range of passion and suffering for which I yearned on this dock.

Thank you, I say to my great-grandparents. Thank you for providing us with the house, to my grandmother for the Sabbath grace earned by her hard work, packing and unpacking, cooking and cleaning, the perpetual domestic round that is invisible to children. Now I wish I could ask her: Was it you who changed the sheets on all the beds? Who swept the floors, who stocked the house with food as we came and went, taking whatever we pleased from fridge or cupboard? Who mopped the bathroom that all of us used, traipsing in and out in dripping bathing suits?

Yet in my memory, my grandmother sits, completing in ink the double crostic whose clues were indecipherable puns, tracing in Hebrew each week's Torah portion on Sabbath afternoons, embodying in her virtuosity the nature that none of us quite inherited, that immense mind with its cerebral esteem for Judaism's nobility and lucid belief in faith and family.

The cottage, whose allure to in-laws was unfathomable, whose lack of hot water and, later, a shower made those who had not been children here so eager for Sunday night, was heaven to us. The word "Bobcaygeon" signified freedom, a house where no one cared if you put your bare feet on the furniture, if you removed all the cushions from the porch couches and chairs to homestead on a rainy day, snug in your soft-sided hut while the summer rain pecked at the screens and turned the gravel, briefly, into jewels.

Ora respects and yet cannot understand the sway of the cottage over us, but I do not need to say a word to Nat and my mother. They grew up swimming across the river, churning ice cream on the porch, composing a newspaper of daily events for their father, at work in a far-off city. Until recently I could leaf through the original hand-pasted editions. Since my grandmother died, no one knows what happened to them.

When I look up, I see my children, Ella in her sailor's jersey, Jake beside her. I kneel low to photograph the boathouse across the river, the greenhouse lawn, the stones beneath the water on which my grandmother stepped gingerly — low enough so that the bridge will not be in the frame. In my mind, the songs of that summer begin to play: Joni Mitchell's "I Think I Understand." Laura Nyro's "Timer."

As I climb the stairs, my mother joins the family

portrait. She tells us that the woman has no problem with our going down to the dock, as long as we keep an eye on the children.

In a baffled tone, my uncle says, "I don't know why I mind" — that we sold the cottage twenty years ago.

How much worse it would have been if my grandmother had not been able to sell, I remind him, in a facsimile of maturity. She was nearly eighty. The family was uneasy about her staying by herself for two summer months. Cousins were older, in camp or Israel; aunts were busy. There was no one to keep my grandmother company.

Yes, Nat acknowledges. "But somehow that's not the point!"

I am unreasonably happy to find that my sensible uncle can also be waylaid by loss.

Now everyone joins me to take pictures from the dock. I look through my camera across the water. Each image — the boathouse, the lawn, the width of the river across which we swam, the marina, the beckoning lake — stands for all that has gone. Like the light on the dock, an eastern sun that drenched us until lunchtime on the Sabbath and then disappeared, leaving us slightly pensive for the rest of the long afternoon, our childhood conferred upon us the sense that even now, in early or late mid-age, we can step back and, in an instant, assume the selves we were.

I say to myself in wonder, "I have come back to Bobcaygeon and may never see it again." But instead of dejection, I feel only thanksgiving. I will not need to return. And perhaps I do not want to. We who have loved it lend this place much of its luster, for without a past to anoint the road and river, the reports of the town's changes were not wrong in their literal description.

My aunt declares that she will not go on. She has walked this far on sufferance, propelled by her fellow feeling for us. When we climb the dock stairs to continue toward the back way, she heads into town. She will meet us on Bolton Street, wherever she can find coffee and a seat.

I remember the back way as a series of winding footpaths linking tiny one-room cottages, like a set designed at children's scale. The people who came out to say hello seemed looming yet benevolent. After walking past the houses we would reach a forest trail, the high light diffused by the cover of branches. If we persisted, trampling twigs and pine needles, sweaty and a little anxious over our increasing distance from the cottage, we could complete the journey, emerging at last before a red lighthouse. Like James at the opening of Virginia Woolf's story, I have to see the lighthouse by day's end.

Almost immediately, however, there is traffic, concrete, heat that is not summery but rebounds from the dark surface of the road. Where are the miniature houses, the pathways, the grasses? The paved road is unforgiving, and cars whip by. Hurrying along the shoulder, I keep glancing behind me, worried about the children's safety.

Bolstered by their juice and chocolate, Jake and Ella are willing to walk all the way, "even if it's far." But we do not reach the lighthouse, for the road is disheartening and the new houses ugly. Only on my right is there a glade through which I can see the river—a dappled scene that reminds me of then, as if a developer had indulged some protesting villager and retained one glimpse of the previous landscape.

In the shadow of the bridge, I find the dip in the road that once led us at night from the cottage down an unforeseen slope to the river's edge, the walk in late summer that my grandmother and I would take before bed.

There is a nocturnal enchantment to my memory of those walks, the hovering moon, the rarity of being alone with my grandmother, the poignant beauty of the evanescent season. In the peaceful silence between us, I felt her great mind harmonizing the pregnant orb and brilliant country stars with the profound atomic understanding of a physicist and the romance of a lover of Wordsworth.

I have not traveled here sentimentally, for I knew the town would not be the same. And although I am thrilled that my children have seen Bobcaygeon, I am under no illusion that, at nine and five, they will remember much. All I am able to say is: I had to see Bobcaygeon one more time.

As we turn back prematurely, agreeing it is pointless to continue, we turn around for good, like many endings not yet encountered but on the horizon, waiting for me.

This awareness is part of an imperfection I can relish now. The children are tired. My aunt has repaired to a cafe. The afternoon is waning; we must go.

I have promised Jake and Ella souvenirs and am willing to spend a considerable sum on kitschy T-shirts, mugs, and other ephemera. Once, in my twenties, in a stylish Italian store, I was complimented by an effete sales clerk on my white shirt, emblazoned with a garish fish and the word "Bobcaygeon."

My mother and Nat look for Ora, as the children and I begin our quest in earnest at the top of the street. Down and down we go, but all we find are postcards. There are sweatshirts with discreet logos saying "Bobcaygeon" that are not nearly outré enough to wear. There are trinkets in a 5 & 10, but none is memorable. Then the children spot a bin of small change purses and become fixated on the same one. Jake found it first, but I want him to defer to his sister; she is five and more likely to use it. He will not yield. Ella weeps and I can console her only with promises of future gifts in whose existence I have little confidence.

We cross the street to the drugstore. Nothing. Walking up Bolton Street, gentrified by hanging plants and wrought-iron benches, we reach a storefront. In the window are my uncle, aunt, and mother, sitting in a genuine cafe — not a coffee shop — dropped in the middle of Bobcaygeon.

The lovely cafe is as much an affront to memory as the back way, although I, a devotee of cafes, think it churlish to deny the worthy residents of this town my favorite activity. And I long to join the others, to rest my legs. But I am under pressure from the children. They do not, they emphasize, want to stay and are already waiting for me outside as I order and hastily drink a latte.

We traipse. Although I have not felt like a pregnant person on the trip, now every part of my body seems to hurt as we walk, the stores closing, one after another, Ella crying, Jake depositing himself on a bench. I begin to worry: Will this trudging be my memory of the journey, the culmination of all the years of reverie — a purgatory of fruitless shopping?

We have looked in a sporty clothing store, declining a necklace and turning down assorted T-shirts and hats. The store of candles and knickknacks is a dud. The handmade-craft store is already shuttered. I am deflated and trying not to lose my temper as I feel a million years old.

What to do? We enter an empty, cavernous restaurant at the corner to inquire if there is another shopping area. There is not. By now, I am attempting to negotiate a deal with Ella, flagrantly bribing her with a more lavish gift when we are back in New York. But she has already been restored to generosity as it becomes clear that Bobcaygeon will not furnish a suitable present for her.

As we drag ourselves back to the houseboat, the air is drizzling. Subdued and damp, we step into the boat. My mother and aunt have thoughtfully prepared dinner, which I eat with hearty gratitude. Hearing the rain on the roof above us, I am inhabited by a very old feeling of sanctuary, of sitting with my grandmother on the porch, the unsynchronized turning of our pages the only sound beyond the rain that speckled the screens, while a bouquet of water, sodden wood, and drenched leaves rose from the river.

Fatigue vanquished, I am elated by a sense of completion so intimate that I do not attempt to put it into words.

We go out into the fading light. The sky over the river, bank to bank, is swept by a double rainbow, two arcs of dazzling translucence that miraculously linger until twilight. We linger, too, amazed by the bounty of two double rainbows in two days, by the reassurance of this most ancient augury.

A sign. I will not see the lighthouse, but when I return to New York and the present — my grandmother dead for a decade, the cottage gone — I will take down, as I do most years, my copy of *To the Lighthouse*. Curled beneath my quilt, the city muted by night outside my window, I will read of a family that dreams through time of light and art and love, the book offering me its trustworthy consolations.

In the boat, my aunt has set up the bed for us. I am struck once more by the pleasing incongruity of her nature. She takes care of herself with unself-conscious clarity about what she does not like to do — cook under pressure, navigate — but her goodness and spontaneous gifts are as reliable as her declared antipathies, which she offers impersonally and cheerfully. How excellent to return to the boat after so long and intense a day and not have to make up the bed!

All of us are worn out by feeling. Getting ready for sleep, I am relieved that the day is over. But there is a last surprise. My uncle has bought an ice cream cake, which he removes from the freezer ceremoniously. The coda to our day has more sophisticated flavors than I expect from a packaged supermarket treat — mocha, macadamia, pistachio. Nat, Ella, and I have a bowl each, while

Jake, a vanilla-only man, says no with the air of someone used to renunciation.

Once again, I wake to the sound of giggling, more prolonged and giddy laughter than usual. It seems that in the middle of the night, my uncle could not get comfortable on the couch, for every time my aunt turned, he had to turn, too.

My aunt protested, "But I have only two positions!"

In the dark, my mother's disembodied voice was heard: "Some people would say that shows a lack of imagination."

Friday

At six-thirty, I step onto the pier to take my leave. I know my uncle anticipates a rush of boats before the approaching weekend, but I need to say good-bye alone. Jake and Ella are still sleeping as I hurry out.

"Don't be long," my uncle calls to me.

In the sleepy morning, I cross the swing bridge, walk past the old post office, over one bridge and then another until I am at Front Street.

And here I must stop. I have been checking my watch in my unleisurely approach and cannot justify the delay I would cause if I walked another ten minutes to the cottage site and then back. Instead, I take my final pictures of Bobcaygeon and race to the boat.

The adults are impatient but not angry. I apologize only half-heartedly: I know Nat understands. He is in charge, steering, as we pull out by seven. It is the last day of the boat trip, and, for the first and only time, we have made an early start.

The boat moves into the middle of the Bobcaygeon River. Good-bye, Gordon's marina. Good-bye, dock. Good-bye, green boathouse and ugly bridge. Turning into Pigeon Lake, we head down to the town of Omemee, where our car awaits us.

We are speeding along as I help the children eat, dress, pack. Suddenly, time is overtaking me. Not a minute to stand on the deck, memorizing green pines and blue water. Not an intentional breath to savor the scent of cedar. Before I know it, we are returning the boat.

Despite the vector from lake to land, from glade to town, from quiescence to motion, we are not quite the same people who left six days ago. Weightless, transparent, we are stripped of precedent, vulnerable to revelation. My practical mother and uncle are more receptive to wonder. Ora finds the world very good. The children are witty for the length of the ride home.

It must be confessed that my tranquil state is seasoned with a sense of superiority, for I did perceive among my husband and sisters some anxiety about whether the trip could possibly assuage such a long-cultivated desire.

As the car bounds down the highway, my smugness turns into anticipation. In returning to the Jewish calendar, we are impelled by time. After we pull into my parents' driveway in Toronto, we will need to shower and prepare for Shabbat, which begins tonight, eighteen minutes before sunset, precisely noted on the refrigerator calendar.

We will rejoin my father, who is waiting for us, embrace my husband, who arrives from New York today, deadlines met, and eagerly join the gathering of my maternal clan for a celebration in the midst of darkening.

My father is still able to recall where we have been and where we are going. Rafe is ill, but on this long weekend before fall, his daughter, my cousin, is getting married. Fittingly, as in the Shakespearean comedies my grandmother loved, this journey will end in a wedding.

After

I T IS MIDNIGHT IN NEW YORK, the time between time. Everyone sleeps. I walk from room to room, organizing homework sheets, turning off the last lights. On my way, I step over the threshold of my daughters' darkened bedroom. Their faces erased of delight and care, they lie above their covers, open-armed, askew. Behind protective bookcases in his room, my son, too, is asleep.

In our bed, my husband sprawls across the quilt, the movie before his closed eyes enticing no one. I extinguish the screen and climb in beside him, nudging him gently, tugging my side of the quilt around me. Lamp on, cloaked in white, I hug my solitude. And then I reach for my book.

After years of sublimation, of socializing myself not to read at the table or in front of people who deserve my entire attention, I have returned to my first passion with the same shocked intensity with which others have affairs or quit their jobs. Lying in bed, propped on my elbows before a library book with its captivating, unstylish cover, I resume my vocation.

"What are you reading?" my grandmother used to inquire in exactly the tone I once heard a woman at a wedding reception ask seductively of another, "What are you drinking?"

My grandmother understood the voluptuousness of reading. Like her, I have loved—and lived—to read. The consequence is that my childhood recalled is not pristine but blurry as I read in the dark, down the stairs, during breakfast, and through school about girl detectives or pioneer children, orphans, witches, maidens, and, most alluring, siblings who accidentally enter other worlds.

Reading was the way I traveled then. How can I describe the sovereignty of print over me, how I stood in the bookstore until I had devoured Nancy Drew's exploits, the latest in a series my mother would not buy—although she conceded that in her youth she had loved them as much as I. I coveted the volumes I had not yet read as if they were a drug, pressuring classmates whose parents were more obliging to lend me their brand-new copies, which I would return the next day after too little sleep.

To open a book and be seduced by the first page, to weep over books until the print danced, to shiver in the backyard through the last daylight because the thought of stopping, even to go inside, could not be borne, to offend my friends when I read their cereal boxes instead of play-ing—all this was paradise.

Among the most disquieting aspects of new motherhood was the recognition that I could no longer read whenever I wanted, could not pick up a book to change my mood or flee my circumstances. I had not re-alized, until I had babies, how much I relied on reading. Now I experienced my yearning as a curse, for my book beckoned always, even when the children needed me. Twice I can remember reading a book from beginning to end, perched on my bedside uncomfortably, because I had intended simply to taste the writer's style, while hours passed and I became aware, vaguely, that the chil-dren were wild with impatience.

When as a child I told my mother that she was using her "hmm" voice as she read while I was trying to talk to her, she laughed and said she remembered well how she sought her mother's attention and was met with the same "hmm."

"I'm the third generation of 'hmm,'" I would say to Jake, who was not amused. One of my sisters defined motherhood as an attempt to pacify the children so that you could finish your book. When I repeat this bon mot to women who do not share my lust for the transport only a book can offer, they look horrified. But women who are readers offer a smile of complicity. I even allocate a role for God, who, I believe, sends me the book that perfectly matches my need when I am desperate.

In the blowsy noon of late August, I can feel the turn of the year in my bones and blood. The unfolding evenings of summer will stop loitering for my pleasure. I will not be able to walk after work by the river. Soon I will be wearing a sweater, and color will leach from the sky before I am ready.

These are the September days, elegiac, lambent. The air has no hint of the shivering it will soon bestow, and yet the blue cut of the light cannot be mistaken for the iridescence of summer.

These are the days I intentionally savor. If I wake on a Sabbath or Sunday to such a day and walk outside with the children, I always say, holding out both arms as if to embrace the world, "It's the last balmy day."

There is usually another after I have said farewell. But unlike summer, whose gorgeous days are profligate, in

September each such day is a gift. Passersby wear sandals defiantly, sometimes looking silly in shorts and tube tops.

Often this weather coincides with the sobriety of the Jewish holy days, when we emerge after many hours of prayer to blink in the ravishing light, then to amble down to the river into which we will symbolically cast our transgressions. We can atone for all trespasses against our Creator, but if we want to atone for acts committed against humankind, only the people we have wounded can forgive us.

In the summer I live in the present, and in the eternal present of all the lyrical summers of my life. No matter how old I become, this is the season that can return me, by the music of water against the stone pier, by a fresh wind on bare skin, to my girlhood or to the time when I first fell in love.

But in September, I am bound to my past in ways both disheartening and restorative. Who is not discouraged by the fact that contrition is required each year because transgression is inevitable? Who has not, in the Ten Days of Penitence between Rosh Hashanah, the birthday of the world, and Yom Kippur, the white fast of absolution, resolved in the morning to be gentle with the children, no matter what the provocation, only to see good intentions undone by a bad night's sleep and a harrowing day?

In the straits of autumn, when I recognize the

darkness in which I find myself but cannot dispel it, I often go to the library. My mother would take us every week, in preparation for the Sabbath. As soon as I could, I made the Friday afternoon pilgrimage.

What exultation reading conferred on my days. Now I cannot find so easily the books that induce such abandon. But when I do, I return to being the girl who could not stop.

It is surprising how protective readers have to be about their ardor. Often I am asked, in a faintly accusatory tone, "But when do you have time to read?" The question provokes the ancient shame about my needing books so badly; the gluttony of a passionate reader remains an embarrassment.

Thea, my little daughter, may grow up to say, as Jake and Ella already do, "Mom, why do you have to read so much?" Or she will lie on the couch, books in a rickety column beside her, so engrossed that she does not hear the call for supper. This is the ideal I offer her siblings.

For despite their protests, they do love books. "Read to me," they will plead, even before I have taken off my coat. When I sit with them at bedtime, a cherished book in hand, I think of my grandmother's pronouncing the words "Our Mutual Friend" with affection; she read Dickens aloud to my mother and her brothers on Sabbath afternoons.

Tonight, in the middle of the workweek, I am reading again the final chapters of *Tom's Midnight Garden*, although I finished the book only twenty-four hours ago. Tom is a boy who has discovered by accident how to go back in time. After his initial perplexity, he thinks about time with sufficient attention to understand its secrets. He can remain in the Victorian garden as long as he wishes, for no matter how much time passes there, in the present no time has elapsed.

The book has been in the house since I failed to persuade either of the children to read it. I do not understand why I was compelled to pick it up, nor why I have thought about the book's ending all day, longing to reencounter its final surprise as Tom craved his own return to the garden. Poised between the day and the morrow, knowing what is about to transpire in these pages, I am still mesmerized. For *Tom's Midnight Garden* is a work of art for children that exacts of its characters no price for knowledge. Although Tom's permanent awakening into the present is so crushing that his cry of anguish echoes across pages written a half century ago into my own midnight, the author has one more reversal in store, most enchanting of all, the reunion within time and despite it.

Which is why on the following night, Jake, Ella, and I are lounging in my room while I read aloud the last six chapters. I know it is late and that Ella should be asleep; I know that Jake will not finish his homework, and that it will take close to two hours until I complete my self-appointed task. But I feel deliciously subversive, upending the routine I myself have established, the staid necessities of weekday existence.

The children lie on pillows, sleepy eyed, enthralled. I have summarized the rest of the book and now, page after page, I bring them into my midnight world. Periodically, I ask each with faux sincerity if I should go on. Their outrage is sanction enough.

When I reach the astonishing moment, almost at the end, during which Tom is reconstituted by joy, I fear that Jake has guessed the surprise. But the gods of reading are kind. He intuits the answer, but he cannot bring it fully into consciousness. And so, when I read the pages that reveal all, my voice shaky with emotion, when my son and my daughter spring up, languor fled, mouths uttering "What?!" and "Oh!" I am incandescent.

For days afterward, I feel redeemed, with its attending trace of immortality. When sorrow approaches, I have only to recall the ending of the book, and the searing imminence of pain is vanquished. I am wrapped in the triumph of literature over life, the opiate of my past.

What hold has this book over me? I speculate: In my forties, when people I love are ill or dead—they never will come back! my childish threnody—Tom's repeal of time, the garden a thought away, the past as present as the moment in which I tell you this story, is a fine solace.

Such solace is genuine but cannot hold at bay the inevitability of suffering. I have taught Jake and Ella that in the Jewish calendar the new day is born paradoxically at dusk. I have explained to them, when they encounter disappointment, that the world is made of light and darkness, and that not one of us can live only in light.

But whether you dissolve into a state of blessing or descend into despair, each seems timeless. It is not possible to hold before one's inner eye the imperative of change. At their most realized, joy and suffering are pure, intolerant of their opposite.

And so, when I returned to New York after the boat trip, I engaged in the customary debate with myself. I wanted to believe that the serenity engendered by the trip partook of an enlightenment that daily life could not undo. I wanted to believe in this exception despite the knowledge earned by any working person, the physics of vacations: Whatever well-being is bequeathed by even the most extraordinary holiday has less force than the press of the quotidian.

Soon enough, the din of work escalated. I longed to speak to my father, who had encountered every kind of quandary as the physician-in-chief of a teaching hospital.

When my sisters and I were small, he kept the burdens to himself, confiding only in my mother to spare us anxiety. As we grew older, his work displaced him from the family. Only now did I wish to probe how he deflected opposition, instilled a noble vision despite distraction, inspired the reverence with which his many students speak of him.

Too late. My father could not know as his four daughters were growing up that his was the wisdom we would need. We, in turn, could not predict that his passion for work would goad each one of us to seek a profession engaging enough to match the eagerness with which he left the house in the morning, the slam of the front door, hum of the opening garage, accelerating motor of the car downtown to the hospital, where matters of consequence would arise each day that only he could resolve. His muddled memory had a diagnosis now, and it was dire, our perplexity yielding to grief.

In New York, the compression of the boat trip gave way to family inflation, as school supplies and fall ephemera proliferated to occupy any empty corner or closet shelf of the apartment. My to-do list expanded drastically, a smirking despot I could not escape. I resigned myself to the tyranny of commitments willingly undertaken that nevertheless embezzled minutes, pilfered days.

Then, without precedent, time revoked its inexorable decree. Instead of receding into a vaguely pleasant past, the journey began to expand, permeating my consciousness, enticing me with its allure, as if it continually awaited me. Through the orbiting seasons, the trip kept consecrating my days, startling me with a crowning measure of rapture during festivities, and offsetting, with its shining presence, the inevitable deflation of my spirit as if to say: Once you were able to dwell within such grace, and so grace will return.

I descend, on my mother's side, from a family that esteems reason above many virtues, but I am a mystic. At a family gathering on Passover, I asked the twenty people in the room whether they believed in an afterlife, however hazy and ill defined. Although almost everyone was an observant Jew, I alone of the blood relations was convinced that the soul lives on, that those who are gone continue to watch over us.

My grandmother, I suspect, would not have had much use for the notion of an afterlife, preferring to find this world the forum for humanity's attempt to replace evil with goodness. She did not waste an instant of cognition on dreams of paradise.

Two years after the boat trip, I fly home for the day to see her youngest son, my uncle Rafe. He is dying. It is a matter of months or weeks: We do not know.

Above the clouds, in the cerulean blue, I am

speaking to my grandmother. Rafe was the little boy with blond curls in the photograph above her bed, the only one for whom she allowed herself to soften. Bub, I tell her, I was not able to say good-bye to you, and I will not make that mistake again.

Of course, I am unsure that this visit will be the last. In the round of the Jewish year, the next Passover is scant weeks away, and I imagine that my uncle will hold on at least until then, when his children will gather in his house from the corners of the earth.

Now that I am a mother, I feel a tenderness for my grandmother that is visceral. Her youngest child is dying, out of order. During the boat trip, Nat told me that on the last day of shivah for Bub, he thought to himself, "At least I'll never have to sit shivah again." In the primitive way of the protective eldest child, he believed his turn was next. Instead, Rafe.

I have no idea what Rafe and I will say to each other, but I am unworried. Throughout the many nights I stayed up until three talking with him and my aunt Nina, we had a longstanding joke about running out of subject matter. If any of us had to leave the room for a second, he or she would enjoin the others, "Don't say anything interesting until I come back."

Beneath my thoughts is an awe-filled humility. Has it come to this? I say to myself in wonderment. In the beautiful early morning, I understand the many references in our prayers to the foundational idea that only God knows the future: My soul is Yours and my body Yours. For the doctors cannot make predictions. We are in the realm of limitation, of humanity.

"I don't think I could do what Rafe has done," Nat told me on the phone last night in New York, wishing me well. For Rafe has been our teacher, open from the day of discovery about his illness and his prospects, celebrating every hint of joy, candid but uncomplaining about pain, terror, and relinquishment. I suspect that each one of us has learned from him how better to undertake this journey.

Even as I try to be as unsparing with myself as he has been, I remain the child and he my most youthful uncle. How has the time passed? I say, bewildered. Can we really be in the last chapter, the story ending, the past all we will have?

My father, thankfully, cannot retain his own verdict. His brilliance, already dimmed, will flicker until it is doused by the neurological severing of memory's links. But the vast reserves of medical knowledge laid down in his youth are not easily dissolved. Each time he hears Rafe's diagnosis, he shakes his head and makes the same pronouncement. "What a shame. And Rafe the youngest," he states, bereft anew.

In these early days, none of us will read a word

about my father's ailment. But I already know this much: I will never be granted a last, true conversation with my father.

Leaning forward in the cab on the way to Rafe's house, I think I should prepare myself, but for what? Indeed, when I walk in, he is upstairs with an old friend, occupied with the most mundane of chores, his taxes. I talk with Nina easily, waiting until she tells me to go up.

I can see in an instant how much change a few weeks have wrought. My uncle's head hangs almost to his chest as my aunt helps him back to bed. I sit in a chair beside him, as close as I can. He does not have the strength to hold himself upright. Part of me is shocked by his evident decline, and part of me accepting. This is how it looks, I say to myself. This is how it is.

Rafe tells me he envies people who can stand, that everyday activities like walking seem miraculous. His voice is low as he asks me to hand him the water bottle on his bedside table. After I return the bottle to its place, we begin.

"Remember when you were first married and lived down the block from us?" I say.

"You girls used to walk to meet us on Friday nights," he says in return.

Immediately we are in the rhythm of our life together. I remind him how eagerly we waited for his family at Passover, my bedroom ready for guests as I studied

Latin in my sister's room, half focused on declensions, half primed for the sound of the station wagon in the driveway and the excitement of my cousins pouring into our house, the beginning of the holiday.

We recite words from our past that are incomprehensible to anyone else.

"Susie is mistaken for a pillow," I say, the best line of a play his daughter improvised once while I was visiting. His laughter is a croak, but he does laugh.

Or the time he came to see me after months, took one look at my radiant face, and said, "Who is he?" when no one yet knew about a beau.

Rafe changed my diapers when I was born, and now I am a middle-aged woman. "It has been a lifetime of love," I marvel aloud.

I tell him that I remember his playing classical music at my grandmother's house when he still lived at home. Then we must mention Domenico Scarlatti, a mutual passion. I tease him about Vladimir Horowitz's recording of the piano sonatas, which I love and he contends is a dreadful distortion of the composer.

As we evoke the signposts of a shared life, the debt I owe him returns to me, his understanding when I was a teenager and so mysteriously unhappy. My uncle and aunt were not rich, but they had a gift for taking pleasure, for relishing the overlooked wealth of daily life.

"I've been so lucky to know you," I say. "In our anhedonic family, you showed me how to seize the eros."

"Girls need an example of healthy eros," says Rafe.

Growing up in the fifties, I was a devoted student of fatherhood, as nearly all the fathers I knew except my uncles left for work early in the morning, came home late at night, and sequestered themselves from family life but for one designated activity on Sunday.

"You don't sound like a feminist now," he observes.

Rafe was once the liberal I have continued to be, but in the last decade he has unmistakably flipped, admiring "tough love" media figures, to my dismay. Whereas we used to talk about everything, in recent years I have listened to him silently as he enumerated the shortcomings of working mothers (of which I am one) and other close-to-the-bone subjects. At times, especially after I knew he was ill, I saw such adamant declarations as a kind of consolation, a way of shoring up decisions he had made long ago about work and love.

My own decision not to engage in dispute made our conversations harmonious but somewhat remote. Today, however, we have no more time. And so when he tells me I do not sound like a feminist, I answer him emphatically. "If you think I'm going to talk about my feminism today"—we both smile—"I won't go *near* that one!" I conclude.

Which, in our mutual understanding of what we will not say, turns out to be exactly right.

Rafe lies back on the pillow. If in New York I closed my eyes to picture him, he would be wearing what he is now: gray slacks, a plaid shirt, and a blue zip-up cardigan sweater.

"Breathing seems extraordinary to me," he says.

I thought that by the age of forty-six I was capable of gratitude at last, but I see I have more to learn. There is a prayer of thanksgiving that observant Jews recite to God for creating in us the hidden and revealed passages of our bodies: "If even one were blocked or opened, we would not be able to stand before You."

"Food tastes like" — he makes a moue — "nothing!"

Among the giddy points of my long life with my uncle are the hundreds of ice cream sundaes we consumed, drizzling Nina's incomparable hot fudge over second and third helpings of coffee chocolate chip and butter pecan.

He sips again from the bottle, his hand shaking. "I'm so thirsty," he says. "This is my worst day. The lump —"

I want to give him something, to leap over the chasm between my life and his. I put my hand on his stomach and encounter a dense mass. His body and my hand meet in speechless intimacy.

Then I get up to move beside him.

"You taught me how to say good-bye at Bobcaygeon," I say, my arm around him. I am crying. "But it turns out I'm really bad at it."

He cries with me.

"What comes after?" I ask him. "Do you think there's anything?"

Rafe shakes his head. My uncle is looking at a horizon line very close to him, one I cannot see, but he remains himself, the scrupulously rational son of his parents.

I remind him that I am the only one born into our family who is convinced there is an afterlife. "I think you get to see everyone you like," I tell him. "And none of the ones you don't."

I know my proposal might be his idea of heaven, but he does not waver.

"Your writing touches me in a very deep place," Rafe tells me instead. "I start to cry before I even read it."

I did not know until this moment that my uncle has read my work. I have been too shy to send it to anyone but my parents. My relatives have been appropriately pleased by my being published, but the constancy of their affection has never depended on it.

Unprepared for Rafe's praise, I am very moved. My uncle can be critical. This is a final gift.

"I wanted to see your children again," he says

suddenly. I have never known if he approves of the way they are being raised. He compliments one of my sisters, the husband of another; I make a mental note to tell them.

Is he tiring? I worry. But I cannot leave yet, knowing what leaving signifies.

"I never said I was Orthodox!" he declares out of the blue, making me laugh.

"Me neither," I agree.

We were brought up to say we were observant Jews, without reference to denomination.

"I refuse to move to the right, even if I have no company," I say with bravado.

Rafe says that in fact we have a lot of company, "but they're afraid. You mustn't concede. If you give in —"

He does not need to finish the sentence. There is nothing as basic to my maternal family's code than our steadfastness in being both observant and worldly, unswayed by the pressure to be more punctilious.

Two hours have passed like silk. I lean over my uncle, placing my hands on either side of his face and my head on his chest. "My beautiful uncle," I say. "I love you. I love you."

I kiss him on each cheek. And then I stand, moving toward the door but always facing him. "I'm leaving backwards," I say, "as if in the presence of a king."

But I must return to kiss him again.

At the door, I call out, "I love you very much."

In a strong, clear voice, Rafe says to me, "I love you very much."

On the following Wednesday night in New York, we are concluding the festive Purim meal, our kin from the area gathered around the table. The telephone rings in the kitchen, and I am the one to answer it.

I need to summon Nat from the living room. I know I must give him a sign of what he is about to hear, so that he will not be utterly shocked, but what do I say? Nat has plane reservations to see Rafe on the coming weekend.

"Toronto." I hand him the phone. "Not good."

As I close the kitchen door to give him privacy, I hear his cry, "Oh, no!" And in the tumult and the weeping and the relaying of news, the grieving starts.

Every year the Passover Seder was the same, and every year, without our knowing it fully, we were blessed. The family gathered around the table, and it was very good. We grew from being the children at the end to the young adults in the middle, goading the little ones into the giggling we remembered.

Then we became the aunts and uncles, and, amazingly, the aunts and uncles became great-aunts and -uncles.

That, too, was good, in the natural order, as the Seder was an ordering of sisters and cousins and husbands and children dispersed among other countries throughout the year, assembling to enter spring together.

The first death out of order is the one that begins the teaching: Not all of us will be around the table. This year, all my parents' grandchildren will be under one roof. But under the roof, too, is sorrow.

When we were young, suffering was young and reversible. This year, suffering is our companion and we do not know its end. At the table, we will rejoice with greater fervor because, like the wine drops on the saucer from a once-full cup, we have in our midst babies but we have death; we have the shore of thankfulness and a sea of heartache.

"*Hinei mah tov u-mah nayim,*" we will sing before we start. "How lovely it is when brothers and sisters dwell together." And it will be lovely, and only Elijah the Prophet knew last year if we would sip on this different night from the cup of anguish or festivity.

Pesach celebrates the new year, not the birthday of the world but its rebirth, not our creation but our re-creation out of slavery to freedom. The struggle this year is to taste redemption in an imperfect world, a world where death does not always pass over our houses. Intrinsic to Jewish creation is separation, of light from darkness, of earth from water, of morning from evening. We are the people of separation, of holiness wrested from darkness over the deep so that we know the difference, always, between sacred and daily, between this night and every other night, between life in this world and the world to come.

Everyone around the table loves this world; no one is ready to separate from the others. Last year, although some were evidently ill and some were not, because of illness all of us were fragile. We prepare most for this holiday, but for the possibility of absence we cannot prepare.

How can we celebrate the gifts we have given each other, the irreplaceable lives that have shaped our lives? How can we remember, as we remember Sinai, the freedom that love has granted us, the love that has ennobled us so that, wherever we scatter, we carry it within us like a portable sanctuary?

We savor everything now, we renew the covenant that has made us, uniquely, the family we are. We see each precious life, like the rainbow of God's promise, begun in earth, ending in earth, but between earth and earth: an arc flung to heaven, rare, glorious. We behold the light of these lives, unimaginably beautiful, and we want the sky to be inscribed with their radiance forever.

Remember the time we took the boat trip to the landscapes of our childhood? Remember all the summers, the cottage, the visits anticipated with such excitement we could not sleep? Remember the reconciliations, the harmony after turmoil, the mended understanding? Remember, we plead with each other, when we laughed so hard at the Seder we were crying?

Now and Then

I AM SITTING ON A GREEN HILL in Ontario, the pond below drenched in noon sun. Behind me, my friend Rose and her children are preparing lunch. The clatter of dishes and cutlery on the porch is a faint accompaniment to my reverie. Louder are the crickets, even at midday, and the occasional bee approaching and retreating in this ravishing summer of the new century.

It is the last week of August, four years since the boat trip. So much living and dying has come to pass. Yet here I sit, alone for a moment before my husband and children return from their foray into town.

Rose is an artist. We, too, have been to town, drinking tea in an outdoor cafe as we plan the work we will write and illustrate together. Naturally, it will be about the past, for we have been friends since we were eight.

I revere Rose, her fair beauty, soft speech, and surprising practicality. With apparent effortlessness, she has given several houses her signature, of light and color and ease. For Rose is the goddess of houses. As soon as she bought this farmhouse, she called to invite me here.

Secretly, I am waiting to become Rose when I grow up, although as we are now forty-eight, the prospect is dimming. When I confess this aspiration to her, she laughs.

When Rose was a child she did not speak much, and I suppose I have accommodated myself to our communion. In later years, she came down to earth, and now we can swoop from grand abstractions to tips on streaking our hair. Rose was the most original girl in our grade. In high school, she wore pins on her socks, her brother's sweater backward, and always had an angelic mane. Her mystique won the heart of the cool, dark boy who became her first love.

Seven years ago, just after Labor Day, Rose called me in New York to tell me he was dead. Suddenly, inexplicably, at the cottage with his wife and daughter, his wonderful body stilled. In our twenties and thirties Rose had encountered him once a year. But he was and would always be beloved.

Rose and I speak often about the intoxication of first love. In our teens, we believed that our radiance was conferred by the lover and so could be revoked. Now, without slighting our chosenness, we know that such vitality is a flickering flame we alone can nurture, stoked by art, by the love we bear rather than the love tendered to us, and by our devotion to our children.

Occasionally, we succumb to wistfulness for those torturous days when we saw ourselves as the dreamy objects of forces beyond our power. Then we remind ourselves how unhappy we were. When I look at Rose, I see her as she is, and she is lovely, but transparent within her shines the girl of then, just as she can retrieve that girl in me. This is the privilege of old friendship, and why we can laugh at ourselves as we fluctuate between rueful confessions of vanity and mortal terror.

The forties, it is said, are the adolescence of middle age. Rose and I flouted our culture and made peace with our bodies, learned to find ourselves beautiful most of the time, vanquished thankfully the exaggerated self-loathing of our youth, the looming flaws that we alone noticed, only to be taken aback in this decade by unfamiliar flesh, by our changing shape and etched lines, and by a sneaking resemblance to our mothers.

Even as we celebrate our daughters as they gaze into the mirror—at the age we were when we invented ourselves—we confront our shifting bodies and try to apply our wisdom to our own altered states.

Frivolous or philosophical, bound to our mutable surfaces or our most profound hypotheses, we often feel the relentless goose-step of linear time, seconds clicking from birth to grave. Rose is the daughter of survivors; her first and middle names are those of her murdered grandmothers. I grew up with many classmates who had no grandparents, with teachers who had eluded the crematoria but were not unscathed. Anyone human jousts with the knowledge of death, but our understanding of what is possible in this flawed world is branded on her parents' flesh and lives in the degraded depths of our imagination.

Sometimes the awareness of depravity lends each minute its tang; at other times, we are defeated by inevitabilities we can scarcely name.

It is this inexorable march, the metronome without music, that was dissolved by the boat trip. Instead, time accrued to itself qualities more pertinent to physics or religion: Six days became all the time in this world and the next—an eternity of time, without before or after.

"An eternal life planted within us" is one way the Torah is described. A month ago, I sat at the funeral of a friend's father, a survivor of the Shoah who was a hero.

That is, he saved four family members by hurling them with his hands from the train bound for the extermination camp, he forged documents in Hungary that rescued hundreds of Jewish lives, and then, when he was betrayed and shipped to Auschwitz, he hoarded his meager bread ration and thrust it through barbed wire to give to emaciated girls from his hometown.

Our friend stood before the mourners, weeping, as he described the man his father was. And I, raised up by my contemplation of such a man, thought: "An eternal life planted within."

These days my sisters and I must be our father's memory. As he parts from the person we have known all our lives—the exceptional healer, renowned for his ability to diagnose the most intractable cases—we struggle to salvage what we can, whatever we are able to learn, still, from him, and what we can reclaim within ourselves that bears his name.

My father cannot pray, but he loves the Jewish people. When I pray, my spirit transcends words, vaulting by their means to a realm past the mortal. I see before me, as if I were nestled in his lap, my father's father, the grandfather I adored who died too young, the one who taught my father what it meant to be an heir.

What do we owe those who came before us?

I can trace my passion for language not only to

my mother's precise and articulate family, but to the centuries of commentators on my father's side, conservators of a legacy that, as priests, they could link directly to Aaron the High Priest, brother of Moses, while they extended the tradition as daring interpreters of sacred text.

"Whoever saves a single life," says a passage in the Talmud, "has saved a world." When I was young, I longed for my father's presence, but as I grow older I have come to understand him. My father sequestered himself after dinner with medical journals because in his determination of what it meant to be a doctor, he would not be worthy of his calling if he did not continually master the research in his field.

My sisters and I comprise a radiologist, a linguist, a lawyer, and a writer. We attribute our drive to the example set by our father, a man who loved to work, who would not temper his standards and was unapologetic about distinction, who obligated himself relentlessly and assumed there was only one way to do a job. This perfectionism is a trait of my father's side of the family, whose members are fastidious in dress, obsessively organized, and even more demanding of themselves than they are of the rest of the world.

My father relaxed by reading biographies. He was compelled by many lives, but the tales that absorbed him most were of the Bloomsbury group. A man for whom duty was paramount, he was nevertheless enthralled by the writers and artists who repudiated the sober expectations of their era in favor of imagination.

One hypothesis is that a child may fulfill the subtext of her parent's dream. My father, a scientist, has a daughter who is a writer. Although he was a public man, he is naturally shy and unconfessional — even to himself. Yet he has been emphatically confident about my work. Every week he would surreptitiously remove my books from their customary places in the neighborhood library and move them to the "We Recommend" shelf.

In an act of creativity that may have determined my fate, my father invented my name. To honor the memory of his mother, Nezia, he anglicized the sound. As I read Virginia Woolf's diaries, it was disconcerting to see my name among her sentences, for she called her sister, Vanessa Bell, "Nessa."

When we are born, God pours into each of us the eternity that partakes of the divine image, each person gifted in unique measure.

What is our task? To pour forth fully, all our lives, whatever measure we were given, to redeem the pledge of our birth, the image in which we are wrought. If, when we die, a mourner can stand before the community and proclaim that the gifts, in all their glory, were spilled forth, can there be any higher purpose to our creation?

The brimming cup, the water through our hands. As it was bequeathed to us, so we must return it, measure for measure, augmented by the beauty of our transience, the pool at daybreak, the waterfall at dusk.

This is aristocracy. And this is our anguish — that everything within, the inextricable light and dark we recognize, the capacity to represent the infinite in pigment or word or deed, may not be sufficiently redeemed before we die.

Rose knows how worthy I think her work, how she renders in silk and paint the abyss into which her family was cast. She reads my words and gives them her meticulous imprimatur. But neither of us can offset entirely the self-doubt of the other, which is the common badge of our humanity.

I want to sit in this chair forever, time suspended in noon bliss, fear banished, the sun melting me into the hill beneath my bones, igniting the water, the blue of the sky brazen in its perfection. I am on Rose's farm, I am sprawled on the dock of the cottage when I was a little girl, and somewhere I am welcoming my grandchildren, for whom I pray I may be a harbor, as my grandmother was to me.

Far beneath me on the road I hear the hum of the car, returning with my family. The table is set on the porch; the corners of the brilliant cloth flap like a flag, summoning me to attention. I do not want to go, but I would not forsake my untidy imminent life for anything, its multiplicity, its abundance, its range of love and complexity calling me up the hill into Thea's embrace, the reports by Ella and Jake, and my husband's query about the progress of our work, which began last night while Rose and I sat by the fire, talking, and resumed as we sipped our tea this morning, writing the first words.

NESSA RAPOPORT is the author of a novel, *Preparing for Sabbath*, and of a collection of prose poems, *A Woman's Book of Grieving*. Her essays and stories have been published in the *New York Times*, the *Los Angeles Times*, and *The Forward*, and have been widely anthologized. Her meditations are included in *Objects of the Spirit: Ritual and the Art of Tobi Kahn*. Her column, "Inner Life," appears in *The Jewish Week*. She was awarded a grant by the Canada Council for the Arts for *House on the River*.